Psychic School
How to Become a Psychic Medium

CRAIG HAMILTON-PARKER

Copyright © 2014 Craig Hamilton-Parker

Previously Titled *Opening to the Other Side – How to Become a Psychic or Medium*.

First published in the USA 2005 by Sterling Publishing Co. Inc.
387 Park Avenue South, New York, NY 10016

All rights reserved.

ISBN-13: 978-1502477989

ISBN-10: 150247798X

DEDICATION

To our guru Sathya Sai Baba
and all those who teach and live by the Truth.

CONTENTS

	Acknowledgments	I
	Introduction	1
1	**Open Your Mind to the Other Side** What is a medium?	Pg 4
2	**Psychic School** How to set up and run a circle	Pg 18
3	**Quick Ways to Get Started** Psychic art, advance clairvoyance, and other techniques	Pg 29
4	**Sensing Vibrations** Developing the gift of psychometry, and how to sense history	Pg 41
5	**Going Deeper** Meditation, spirit guides, seeing, and sensing the aura	Pg 56
6	**Mediumistic Development** Princess Diana Séance. Giving proof of life after death	Pg 80
7	**Spiritual Investigation** Spiritual walks, dowsing, and ghost hunts	Pg 107
8	**Advanced Teachings** Trance, inspirational speaking, blindfold clairvoyance	Pg 119
9	**Presentation** Demonstrating to an Audience	Pg 126

ACKNOWLEDGMENTS

Many thanks to Vi Kipling for checking factual content and accuracy of the text and for helping to produce the syllabus and teaching material for our Elysium Online Psychic School..

To the memory of a lovely lady.

INTRODUCTION

"If the rich could hire other people to die for them, the poor could make a wonderful living."
—Yiddish conundrum

Even now, after having worked for most of my life as a medium, I still cannot fully explain what happened that Friday night in September 1987. My wife, Jane, and I had only recently met on March sixth of that same year, a date and meeting predicted five years earlier by the spirit world through the mediumship of the internationally renowned British medium Doris Stokes.

Jane is also a medium, and soon into our relationship we were experiencing many strange phenomena. Perhaps it was something to do with the conjoining of our spiritual powers or the energies of the places we chose to visit during our courting, which included Spiritualist churches, séance rooms, and a memorable, mind-boggling encounter with the Dalai Lama. Our auras were most certainly primed with spiritual energy and we both knew that this period of our lives was especially important—a turning point when synchronicity happens and events take unexpected and strange turns.
The president of our local Spiritualist church, where Jane and I had met during one of my public demonstrations of mediumship, had arranged for us to exorcise poltergeist activity causing trouble on a converted fishing boat. It was moored on the river Hamble in Hampshire, England, close to the ancient site where King Henry VIII once built his navy vessels from the oaks of the New Forest. Anticipating the following night's plan to cross the dark river and board this strange ghost ship, we tried to relax and get some sleep at about 11:00 p.m. Suddenly we were startled bolt upright by an explosion of blinding light in the center of the room. "My God! What's

happening?" Jane called out, as the light proceeded to fold in on itself and hover in a luminous ball, then expand to form a circle of light in the center of the room. The circle was about four feet across and at eye level.

We stared, like startled animals caught in a car's headlights. My immediate thought was that it was lightning—perhaps even ball lightning—but we were indoors and it was a clear evening with no threat of thunderstorms. Yet the room certainly had an electric atmosphere; I could feel the hairs on my arms standing on end.

Jane and I sat speechless as the light hovered for what seemed then like an eternity but could only have been about thirty seconds. Then the circle reformed into a tight ball and shot across the bedroom and out the door, toward the living room. I leapt out of bed, chasing after it into the adjoining room. But seconds later it disappeared, leaving no trace. The light was no clairvoyant vision, or "inner knowing," but as real as this book you are holding. It was tangible, but with no explanation. Jane and I were astonished. Our limbs felt strangely heavy and we were both slightly nauseous.

I believe that what we experienced was linked to the fact that we were both, at that time, living in a highly charged spiritual state. Maybe a protective angelic force was revealing itself in preparation for our encounter with the poltergeist the next day; I don't know. The fact that we felt slightly sick afterward could imply that the energy had something to do with our bodies, perhaps a spontaneous projection of some form of ectoplasm—the invisible substance sometimes produced by mediums and made luminous by spirit communicators.

At another level, the circle is symbolic. The psychologist Carl Jung referred to it as an archetypal image—an inherent primordial idea charged with emotion; a universal symbol common to everyone. A circle is, after all, the simplest form of a mandala (from the Sanskrit meaning "magic circle"), representing the wholeness of the self. Being made of light, it would imply transcendence and divinity.

The circle of light appeared at a spiritually significant time for us, partly because we were in love but also because our mediumistic powers were beginning to work in tandem with one another. It was a time when powerful and transforming forces operational in our lives would soon bring Jane close to death and see me give up a lucrative directorship in advertising to seek a new and uncertain career as a full-time Spiritualist medium. Whatever caused it, the circle of light was for me a marker, coming at a time in my life when everything was changing. In retrospect, it was a signpost to a new direction for both of us, away from material goals and toward new lives—as professional mediums.

In the years that followed, in addition to holding demonstrations, I was encouraged by the spirit to teach mediumistic development in Spiritualist churches, workshops, psychic organizations, and through my writing. Eventually it led me to form my own circle. During those sessions I passed along teachings and instruction to individual members and to the circle as a whole. Some of these are included in the chapters that follow. The guides called the spiritual work we were doing "circle of light," hence the adoption of their term as the title of this book.

The circle of light has since expanded to embrace a great many people into its circumference, one result of my website, which has brought together mediums from around the world who share their teachings. Together we have synthesized American, Australian, British and other Spiritualist methods and developed a system that allows people to learn through chat rooms and by correspondence course. Many highly skilled mediums and wonderfully inspired people have worked together to maintain our online circle of light, called *The Psychics and Mediums Network*. Together we have seeded spirituality in the most unlikely of people, using some of the easy-to-understand methods described in this book together with a series of email teaching modules designed in conjunction with our "headmistress" and Spiritualist medium, Vi Kipling.

Our work together on the Internet has revealed to us that the circle of light is a real spiritual energy that takes no notice of distance and links people together in a fellowship of learning. Together we are being inspired by the spirit to expand our inner light and share our insights with others in a spirit of cheerfulness and compassion. I anticipate that as you work with this book you may join the energy of the circle and perhaps feel our influence and the closeness of those working with you from the spirit world.

1 OPEN YOUR MIND TO THE OTHER SIDE

"It is an old maxim of mine that when you have excluded the impossible, whatever remains, however improbable, must be the truth."
—Sir Arthur Conan Doyle

While I was in India, someone told me an amusing true story about an American who was hoping to speak to his guru. He soon discovered that this was not as simple a feat as he had thought. He was told he would have to wait until he was called from among the thousands of devotees gathered in the ashram, and may not get an interview with the guru at all.

Eventually it was indicated that the guru would speak with the visitor, and the American was invited into the interview room. Upon sighting the guru, however, he blurted out, "I've traveled all the way from America and been kept waiting nearly seven days to see you!" The guru smiled and, with a twinkle in his eye, replied, "And I've been waiting for you nearly two thousand years!"

Clearly, we need to be patient when it comes to spiritual matters. Spiritual insight unfolds when the time is right. Just as the guru appears when our heart is ready, so too our spiritual powers only unfold at the right time. It is our soul that sets the celestial alarm clock, and because of this you will instinctively know when the time is right for your own spiritual development. When the call comes, events will conspire to lead you along the right path and bring you to the right teachers, those with the most suitable teachings for you. The truth will draw you like a magnet.

Is the time right for you to develop your latent powers? Perhaps strange coincidences and phenomena have already been happening to you. Maybe you have had common psychic experiences, such as knowing who is on the other end of the phone when it rings or having dreams that come true. You may be aware of the good or bad vibrations of a building or the energies surrounding another person. You may have seen a ghost or had the spirit of someone you love come to you at a time of crisis. Perhaps you can anticipate what someone is going to say or somehow know which of the people you meet in daily life will be successful or fail in the future. You may have traveled outside of your body, in your spirit body. It is likely that psychic powers are already at work in your life and making themselves known to you through your gut feelings, dreams, and perceptions.

Psychic powers occur spontaneously in millions of people. Yet only a handful go on to develop their psychic gifts, and fewer still will progress to strengthening their mediumistic powers. There's a saying: One person in a hundred may become psychic, but only one in a million may become a medium. You don't choose to become a medium, it just happens. When it does, coincidences occur. You may have bought this book out of curiosity, or you may have sensed something "bigger" driving you. In which case, our meeting through these pages may be no coincidence.

People who have set foot along the path to mediumistic development claim that events conspire to lead them to the people, methods, and philosophy that are needed. Usually a teacher crosses their path. Perhaps you are drawn to a medium who is prepared to provide instruction, or your path leads you to an organization that holds the exact knowledge you seek. Very often an upsetting experience opens doors for you. Many are set upon the path because of bereavement, illness, or a situation they are unable to face. Sadly, adversity is often the catalyst that ignites a spiritual quest.

Should that be the case, it would seem that your heart has heard the call from your soul. I am hoping that this book, and my words, will help you to discover for yourself the wonderful spiritual inheritance that can be accessed through mediumship. And I am hoping that you will learn to use and strengthen these powers in the service of others, so that the light cast may be pure and shine far into the darkness of this materialistic age. Mediumship is a divine calling, requiring you to stop and examine your heart before proceeding. For it is, indeed, a holy office.

In my own case, I did not particularly want to be a psychic medium. As soon as I sat in circle, however, I realized that this was something that was supposed to happen in my life. Yes, there were times when I rejected the gift, and in anger cursed the fact that I was a medium. It was making me too sensitive and had turned my material life upside down. But even when I felt despondent, or wished I had not started out on the path, something would always happen to remind me of the importance of the work. This would often come in the form of a "chance" meeting with someone I had helped, who would tell me how my mediumship had changed his or her life—and sometimes even saved it. I would be reminded of how much good this work can do for others and the joy it can bring into this world. These serendipitous reminders also helped me to see the bigger picture. Today there is nothing I enjoy more than a vibrant public meeting to demonstrate my mediumship and see the suffering of those bereaved lifted by the knowledge that the joy of living never ends.

HUMAN VALUES

Becoming a medium brings with it responsibility. Many people start the process of development but fail in their efforts or give up once they discover the level of dedication required. Have you asked yourself what is really driving you and why you are thinking of becoming a medium? Ask your inner voice to give you guidance, and it will always oblige. Put the question to your soul and it will reply. Remain inwardly silent and in an expectant yet calm mood and just wait for the response that is sure to come. It will come to you via your intuition—perhaps as an inner voice, in the form of a symbolic picture, or just a strong sense of knowing. Now spend a little time contemplating what you have received. The first message that comes through is the right one, as secondary messages may be influenced and changed by your own hopes, expectations, preconceptions, fears, and so on.

Asking your intuition for guidance, and then acting upon it is an easy way to begin accessing your hidden powers. It is a numbingly simple technique, but it is surprising how few people listen to that inner voice. If you want to become a clairvoyant or a medium, you will need to listen to and trust your inner voice, for it is from that quiet place that all the other powers spring. Indeed, I would argue that the inner voice—and particularly the part we call the conscience—is our link not only with our unconscious and the spirit world but also to God. We all have this inner voice—not just mediums.

I hope that the reply you received to your question had something to do with compassion and helping others, rather than personal power or material gain. Today mysticism is an industry, and there are many who seek to develop these powers for the wrong reasons. Are you perhaps motivated by curiosity, power, egotism, or looking for fame? Or do you see yourself helping the bereaved, lifting the clouds of pain and bringing succor to those in need? What sacrifices are you yourself prepared to make? What if your development takes many years? Do you have the stamina and perseverance needed to complete the work?

I'm reminded of a newcomer to a circle who took me aside and said, "Craig, I have been sitting now for six weeks and I am still not getting anything correct. It is my intention to do this for a living, so how much longer is it going to be before I can start charging people?" Clearly the man's motive was not selfless, and his psychic powers never did open up while he sat with me. Others in the same circle, whose motivation was to help others, found their mediumship blossoming quickly.

FINDING YOUR PATH

I now run a closed circle—as opposed to an open circle, which anyone can join—and I particularly like to train young mediums. I am intrigued by the strange coincidences that often accompany a sincere person's decision to seek out a circle. I am sure spirit takes a hand, but it also seems that events conspire to bring people together.

Daren Stephens for example, joined me after a private consultation with my wife, Jane, who identified his latent powers when she gave him a reading in which she connected to his grandmother in spirit. "The reading with Jane completely blew me away," said Daren. "It went on for three hours, and within the reading Jane said I was going to be in a circle and work in front of an audience. I had no intention of becoming a medium but I joined Craig's circle anyway and learned psychometry and mediumship. I am now amazed that I can stand in front of an audience and give accurate proof of life after death! Perhaps the spirit had it all planned out for me!" Accompanying Daren in the circle is his partner, Sue Brooks, who is also developing mediumship and has an uncanny ability to get both the Christian and surnames of the spirit communicator..

Steinar Lund also joined my circle. He has been illustrating my books for some years and is now developing his skills as a psychic artist. Joining him is Christine, her friend Chrissie and Christine's sister, Haley. "I was always aware of something other than our world, but through fear of the unknown I used to ignore it," said Christine. "I had a reading with a very good medium and she insisted that I should get myself into a circle. She handed me a copy of *Psychic News* and told me to look through it. I looked and saw Craig's circle advertised, but couldn't convince any of my friends to go with me.

"I remember watching a demonstration on a TV program called *This Morning* that featured three mediums being tested on air. This gave me the additional push I needed and I decided to go to the circle by myself that evening. When I arrived I realized that it was actually Craig who I had watched on TV earlier that day. Sitting in the circle for the first time I was told that I was pregnant, which I did not expect in the slightest. A test the following day confirmed this. Then, after seeing one of Craig and Jane's publicity photos, I realized that Craig's book was the very first psychic book [*The Psychic Workbook*] that I had purchased a couple of years earlier."

Pretty much everyone who has sat in my circles has felt a similar tug from the spirit. People of like mind but with very different backgrounds are drawn together when a circle is formed. One of the most interesting stories comes from my circle member Phillipou Cornick, an ex-boxer who fought under the name "Wild Man of Borneo." He has influenced many members of the circle to improve their health—including teaching Steinar and me how to box!

Phill's life was turned on its head when his wife, Kaye, died after a long fight with cancer, leaving him to bring up their two children on his own. "I woke up this one morning about three months after her passing and felt absolutely at a loss, empty, everything was black. It was as if my will to live had left me. I felt that I did not really want to be here, it just all seemed so pointless. The other part of me, the part that gave me so much reason to live and so much joy, purpose, and happiness, was now gone from my life. Kaye was everything to me. It was only because of my daughters that I did not take my life to join my beloved."

Soon after this low point, Phill began his search to see if he could contact Kaye's spirit. He visited a number of Spiritualist churches but was never given evidence that convinced him. "That morning, by chance, I opened a book in the library by the Eastern mystical teacher Gurdjieff, and the few lines I read hugely inspired me to continue my search for the truth," Phill said. "Gurdjieff's words leapt out of the page with a bolt that was so powerful that I felt it was awakening memories from a past life. I had an overwhelmingly strong feeling that today I would get the proof I needed from Kaye. I mentioned the fact to my daughter as I left for Gosport Spiritualist Church to watch the medium Craig Hamilton-Parker.

"Before his demonstration Craig gave a talk about philosophy and, to my amazement, within the discourse he spoke about Gurdjieff and said things that corresponded word for word to the teachings I had read earlier that day in the library. During Craig's demonstration he told me various things about my relationship with Kaye that were all accurate. In fact, I would say that the information Craig gave me was almost one hundred percent correct except for two errors. He said that my oldest daughter, Clare, had bleached blonde hair (her hair was not bleached blonde, she was a natural blonde) and that my other daughter, Christalou, had been having problems at school. This was also completely wrong. I had asked Christalou only a couple of nights before if everything was okay at school and she emphatically told me that she was doing fine.

"When I got home I told my daughters about the messages Craig had given from their mum. I told them what he'd got right and also mentioned the two things he had gotten wrong. Christal, my youngest daughter, burst into tears saying, 'Dad, I secretly helped Clare to bleach her hair a few days ago. And about school: I have been finding it difficult because of Mum.' She said she just could not do it anymore and had been very upset only the day before in class. This pierced my heart and I took her in my arms and held her while she sobbed.

"Craig had given me the proof I needed. He could not have been picking up messages telepathically from me because I did not know this information until after the demonstration, when I spoke to my daughters about it. He only could have picked up the information from some other source outside of himself and outside of me. It must have come from Kaye!

"Finding this out made my heart jump for joy, and from then on my life took on new meaning and vigor. I explained to Christal that "Mum wants you to do well at school because the fact that she gave this information through Craig proves that she is watching over you." It made her feel better, and after this talk her attitude at school changed back to what it was when Kaye was still with us. Christal could cope again.

"Soon after, I found out that Craig was setting up a circle. I felt that I too wanted to learn and maybe I could also enrich people's lives one day. I joined his circle and have not looked back since. Of course, I still think of Kaye and sometimes I still miss her, but now the grief has turned into a warm and loving memory. Five years later, I just call her from my heart and I will either see her in my dreams or in the stillness of my mind. I know that she is with me."

BECOMING A MEDIUM

Developing mediumship requires the qualities of integrity, perseverance, morality, and, above all, compassion. However, not all mediums are spiritual or ethical. I have met mediums with low morals and high egos. I have even seen known fraudulent mediums, who have in the past been exposed by Spiritualists, working on television. Sometimes the flower of mediumship blooms on strange soil, but the human values and qualities of character I have spoken about are present in the majority of mediums. Before we progress, it is important to clarify exactly what I mean by a medium. Mediums are people who have a special gift that allows people in spirit to give them messages from the afterlife. She or he is the link between the two worlds, communicating with people who have died through mind-to-mind contact (telepathy). The objective of a medium's work is to prove survival of the human personality after death and to help the bereaved come to terms with their loss.

The medium may produce enough information to satisfy inquirers that a family member, friend, or loved one still survives death. The medium may, for example, give an accurate physical description of the deceased, their work, anecdotes from their earthly life, what illness they died of, and so on. Only after the identity of the spirit person is clearly established, will the medium give further evidence about shared and past memories related to current events in the sitter's life. In addition, the medium may give extra details, such as information about hobbies and idiosyncrasies that can help establish the personality of the communicator.

It is important to differentiate mediumship from psychic counseling and fortune telling. A psychic is a person who has extrasensory perception— also known as ESP or the sixth sense. These gifts include telepathy, clairvoyance, precognition, and sometimes psychokinesis. Although a medium will have the same gifts, the psychic does not have the ability to give verifiable information about spirit communicators. A psychic is able to "sense" on a material level, but is not able to reliably "tune in" to the spirit world, except by accident.

Some of us call ourselves "psychic mediums" because we have mediumistic ability and also powers of clairvoyance and prophecy. It is, however, unwise to mix prophecy and mediumship. In British Spiritualism, the medium is forbidden to make predictions, restricting him or her to providing verifiable information to prove that life exists after death. Through the mediumship of the trance medium Emma Hardinge Britten, Spiritualists were given seven principles that became the bedrock of their beliefs. One of these was personal responsibility. Taking personal responsibility for our lives implies that we have free will when deciding our future.

Psychic powers are very widespread and everyone is psychic to some degree, if we use the natural intuitive or sixth sense inherent in all of us. In order to become a medium, it is necessary to first develop the basic psychic powers. I will be talking you through these stages to mediumship in this book.

Qualities Needed for Mediumship

We have already established that it is important to have patience when developing your gifts and to recognize that the path requires the spiritual qualities of integrity, morality, and compassion. You also may have experienced suffering in your personal life, so you will have empathy with the suffering of others. Given that you have these qualities and a latent gift, with work your powers may begin to unfold. This will not happen all at once, but over a period of time. Sometimes you will make great strides and surge ahead very quickly, at other times the path may seem steep and slow. But it is all part of the same journey. Keep going and never loose faith in yourself.

Faith in yourself is vitally important in the success of any enterprise. An entrepreneur has faith in him- or herself but, as success comes, he or she may become arrogant and self-centered. It is sad to see self-confidence turn to arrogance, for instead of drawing the admiration of others, the person will only receive our scorn. These changes are not the qualities you would expect to find in a medium, yet it is an endemic problem.

To prevent arrogance from rearing its ugly head, we need to temper self-confidence with modesty. Do this right from the start, and your mediumship will grow to become both accurate and spiritual. Too many mediums fall victim to what in Greek tragedy is called hubris, that is overbearing pride, presumption, and arrogance, which eventually results in disastrous situations. In mythology, the hero often falls at the last hurdle because of his pride. Hubris is defiance, arrogance, thinking you can outsmart the gods. It was at work when Oedipus refused to believe that he had killed his father and married his mother; when Creon insisted on leaving the body of Polynices to rot in the fields; and when Odysseus's crew slaughtered the sacred cattle of the sun god Apollo.

It is the same with inner work. The would-be medium must fathom his or her unconscious to discover his or her intuitive self, and even though personal spiritual treasures will be discovered it is vitally important to remember that the powers that come are not ours: They are on loan from God. Tell people what a brilliant medium you are to instill confidence, even brag in a humorous way about being so fabulous, but in your heart remain humble. Remember, too, that self-righteous modesty is also arrogance. Have fun and joke about your gift, but take yourself too seriously deep down and you are lost. People may praise you, even idealize you, but you must remember always that you serve at the pleasure of God. We are servants, and it is an honor to do this work. It is we who must remain forever grateful.

Measuring Psychic and Mediumistic Gifts

The American researcher Joseph Banks Rhine is considered the father of serious scientific research into the paranormal. In the 1930s, at Duke University, in North Carolina he undertook the first systematic study of the subject and used statistics to quantify his exhaustive tests. Together with his colleague Carl Zener, he designed a set of cards imprinted with colorful geometric symbols, which were used in various card-guessing games. His conclusion was that many people guessed correctly far more times than one would expect from chance alone. That meant they were receiving information from something other than the known five senses. Rhine defined this sixth sense as "extra sensory perception," and subdivided it into four basic abilities:

- **Telepathy:** the ability to "tune in" to the thoughts of others or to inject your own thoughts into another's mind.
- **Clairvoyance**: the power to see things not visible through the known senses and not known by anyone else.
- **Precognition:** the skill of looking into the future and seeing events before they take place, often through the subconscious while in the dream state.
- **Psychokinesis:** the ability to use the power of the mind to influence matter—to move objects by thought, for example.

Personality Traits of Mediums

Parapsychologists have shown that psychic and mediumistic people share certain qualities, and this may account for why some people are more psychic than others:

Personality. Psychic people are usually extroverts. Tests guessing the turn of random Zener cards have shown that outgoing individuals score better than somber, reflective types. Psychic researcher Betty Humphrey, from Duke University, discovered that extroverts displayed stronger ESP abilities than introverts. Psychics and mediums usually are also cheerful people. In 1977, researcher John Palmer examined every single published experiment on neuroticism and ESP. He demonstrated that highly neurotic people were poor ESP subjects, while optimists received better results.

It has also been found that psychics and mediums enjoy taking risks, and that gamblers and other risk takers display higher ESP abilities. Perhaps some may also be able to influence the fall of dice by psychokinesis.

Sensitivity. Psychic and mediumistic people are usually extremely sensitive individuals, often influenced by other people's moods. You may be able to tell that someone is in a bad mood even before you actually meet or see it in his or her face.

Psychic and mediumistic powers also appear to work best when the people working together actually like one another—or, better still, love one another. The telepathic bond between siblings or parents and their youngsters has proven to be especially strong. Experiments have shown that a mother's heartbeat increases when her baby wakes and cries—even if the child is in a soundproof room or at another location.

Creativity. A large proportion of psychic and mediumistic people come from artistic backgrounds. I was an artist for many years, and many of my mediumistic friends have an artistic gift. Some can even draw portraits of the spirit people they see. Some researchers believe that psychics and mediums, like artists, have a highly developed right brain—the side of their brain responsible for intuition. Imaginative, creative people—particularly artists—score better in ESP tests than systematic thinkers.

Many psychic people can visually project imagined images into random shapes. Scrying, sand reading, and tea-leaf reading all employ this technique.

Dreams. Psychic and mediumistic people will often have lucid dreams—dreams that are so vivid that you feel you are conscious while the dream is taking place. Dreams connect us to the unconscious mind and its psychic intuition. Psychic experiences are most likely to happen when the mind and the body are relaxed and receptive. Measurements of brain waves indicate that a person who is dreaming or meditating emits wave patterns similar to those of a psychic demonstrating his or her skills. (A physicist, Julian D. Isaacs from John F. Kennedy University in Orinda, California, researched brain waves by mapping them as the subject was giving a demonstration of ESP, such as bending spoons using psychokinesis.)

The first ESP experiences of many of people occur in dreams, and I have written a book about this entitled *Psychic Dreaming*. In dreams, we may see the future or the distant past. We may meet our friends, talk to the dead, and sometimes be able to psychically perceive distant locations through clairvoyance— an ability dubbed "remote viewing" by the CIA, who employed psychics to spy on Soviet installations during the Cold War.

Perceptions. It has been suggested that the pineal gland, which is about the size of a pea and lies in the center of the brain, may have something to do with our clairvoyant ability. It is thought by some to be the vestige of a reptilian eye from the time of the dinosaurs, and, as it is in a direct horizontal line with the center of the forehead, may be the "third eye" spoken about in mysticism.

The ancient Greeks believed the pineal gland to be our connection to the "realms of thought." Descartes called it the "seat of the soul."
Modern scientists have discovered that the production of a chemical in the pineal gland, called serotonin, is disrupted when a person takes hallucinogenic drugs such as mescaline or LSD. And therefore, it is believed that the gland is a significant factor in the mystical experiences claimed to be triggered by hallucinogens. As the pineal third eye is related to seeing light, it may, in fact, be the source of the "inner light" of mystical experiences and of altered perceptions, such as seeing the aura, that are experienced by psychic people.

Psychic and Mediumistic Eccentrics

All of the above may help scientists to form a profile of psychic and mediumistic people, but certainly not all mediums are highly sensitive extrovert artists with eyes like lizards. If you know any mediums personally you will appreciate that it takes all sorts to make the psychic world. Mediums who work with the media, such as John Edward, Van Praagh, and Jane and myself, give very polished presentations, which can sometimes mask the quirkiness of our natures. I love the eccentricity of many mediums, and within Spiritualism you will meet some extraordinary and adorable personalities who would probably horrify most TV producers!

So if you do not share all of the personality traits described above, don't worry. It takes all sorts. I have seen mediums who have a habit of spitting out their false teeth halfway through a message, others who shout in such a loud voice that it makes you jump, one who would take her wig off without warning, and some that get their words so mixed up that the resulting double entendres are hugely embarrassing. I particularly love the way mediums mix up their words when they are engrossed in their mediumship. My wife, Jane, has dropped some wonderful malaprops and plays on words.

I've caught her saying things like "decapitated coffee" and "bitten to death my midgets." My personal favorite was a reference she made to a movie, "Jason and the Juggernauts."

What a Medium Does

I have already written about what differentiates a medium and a psychic. Many people call themselves mediums but they are in reality psychics. As there is a great deal of misconception about what exactly a medium does, I will briefly explain.

We give proof:
A medium gives proof of survival of the personality after death. We demonstrate that not only does the life essence continue but also that memory and self-awareness—the sense of being who we are—persists. The information a medium provides may bring comfort to the bereaved and help them to move forward. Some describe this process as a form of soul healing. Sometimes a spiritual healing gift that helps to heal the sick will accompany the awakening mediumistic gifts.

We are a link between the worlds:
This has sometimes been described as being like a telephone operator who makes the call then relays the information received to the person on the other end of the line. The quality of the line can vary occasionally and may "crackle" if inappropriate conditions or negative thoughts from participants break the "signal." We are intermediaries working in a spirit of service and not the possessor of spiritual power.

We connect to a higher philosophy:
With the help of our spirit guides and spirit helpers we can share in the wonderful philosophy given to us from the next world. The spirit guides may eventually be able to channel philosophy through a medium by means of inspired talks and trance. If the medium has creative talents such as writing, music, or artistic skills, then these may be used in spirit communication. However, before we can give evidential spirit messages we must first know how to link, through meditation, to the spirit within in order to truly understand the enduring philosophy of compassion.

We enable spiritual growth:
Mediumship and the knowledge it brings will probably inspire us to become better people ourselves. We may allow our intuition to integrate with our reason, become more sensitive and tolerant, and be willing to learn from many sources. A good medium will continually want to learn more and

keep pushing his mediumship forward. Our expanding knowledge and gifts will inspire others to make the best of their lives.

We help one another to discover God:
Mediumship is a spiritual gift that proves the existence of an afterlife. Mediumship implies that there is a God but does not necessarily prove the existence of God. Some mediums believe in a personal God and may follow traditional faiths, including Christianity, whereas others may believe God to be the omnipresent force of love. My experience of the philosophy given from spirit encourages me to look at the ways religions are similar rather than the ways in which they differ. In all of them are echoes of a universal religion that transcends race, creed, and dogma.

AN EXPERIMENT TO TRY

Creative Visualization:
Imagine Being a Medium

Successful athletes are those who can "see" themselves winning. Psychologists believe that this ability to visualize a goal actually changes the physical structure of the brain and builds initial learning pathways that make achieving the goal easier. Visualization creates the first tentative connections between the neurons of the brain that eventually become the well-trodden pathways of learned habit.

In the next chapters I will be giving you specific techniques that will enable you to develop your psychic and mediumistic powers. Just like a successful athlete who "sees" his or her success, you, too, need to have a "vision" for your mediumship. Before we progress, let's spend a little time encouraging our subconscious to set up the pathways to spiritual insight:

Imagining yourself working as a medium. Create in your mind's eye a positive image of yourself doing private sittings, speaking from the platform, or whatever method appeals to you. Select the situation you hope for and now feel that you are there. Look around and become aware of the people enjoying your presentation. You can hear their positive comments and encouragement. You can also see yourself overcoming difficult situations when you thought the mediumship was not coming through. Remind yourself to be confident with your gift and you'll need never feel dejected. Be aware of the cheerful feelings that come with using humor, compassion, and optimism in your mediumship. Build a positive image of yourself achieving accurate mediumship.

Now notice how the spirit world is connecting to you. They will use all of your senses to make their communications. Think about hearing the spirits working with you. This could be an inner voice or, for this exercise, you may imagine hearing a real voice. You are able to recognize genuine spirit contact.

Many of the impressions that come from the spirit are impressed upon your body to communicate qualities of the person communicating. Consider what it will be like when a spirit draws close. How would it feel to become aware of being a big person or someone with a small frame or maybe someone of the opposite sex?

How do you think the spirit world would communicate the sense of smell? Working with the all the perceptions will help you to see, feel, and hear the spirit communicators. Also be aware of how character, feelings, and mood can be communicated.

Using your imagination in this way establishes a subconscious success pattern. It will help to build your confidence as well as help you to understand the inner processes that accompany mediumship. Putting yourself in an imaginary setting, such as in a consulting room or before an audience, will enable you to overcome stage fright or nervousness and lead you toward greater self-confidence should the time come for you to work with groups of people.

Visualization is more than just seeing; it is the art of using the imagination to experience new situations. Regularly practice this exercise in imagery to help build your self-confidence. Make your imagined mediumship a resounding success so that positive affirmations become embedded into your brain and spirit. Your visualization is preparing you for success and simultaneously is sending messages to the spirit to help you with your work.

2 PSYCHIC SCHOOL

"And those who were seen dancing were thought to be insane by those who could not hear the music."
—**Frederick Nietzsche**

Ideally the best way to develop your mediumistic potential is to sit in circle with an advanced teaching medium. The medium will be able to recognize your potential, encourage you to develop, reprimand you when necessary, and show you the techniques and methods needed to unfold your gifts. After sitting with your teacher for and average of 2 to 4 years, you will be ready to take your first steps as a fledgling medium in a Spiritualist church. If you are fortunate enough to have a medium mentor, then this book will serve as a useful complement to the techniques you are already learning. But good teaching mediums are hard to find, so most of you reading this book are either going to have to develop your gifts alone or form a small group with other like-minded, committed people who are prepared to work together.

It is far easier to develop your mediumistic abilities if you can work with a group of between six and ten people with a common objective. You can encourage one another, learn from one another, have others to practice with, and aid each other's progress. Working together will quicken the spiritual growth of each of you in ways that would be hard to achieve on your own, and your collective psychic energy will push you all forward. When people work together in a psychic circle not only do their individual spiritual energies combine but also the spirit guides and helpers from the next world add to this energy, so that the total energy available to the group becomes greater than the sum of its parts. In a good circle the air will buzz with powerful psychic energy.

The bedrock of Spiritualism is the home circle; from these circles developed the communities that formed into churches and eventually into the modern movement. They usually consisted of small groups of friends and family that sat with the common purpose of experiencing phenomena and developing mediumship. Some of the best evidence of survival and most startling physical phenomena came from these pioneer groups that sprang up after March 31st 1848 when two sisters, Margaretta and Catherine Fox, established intelligent communication with a spirit entity which had been responsible for noisy rappings in their home . Many of these first home circles had no medium conducting the proceedings.

FORMING YOUR GROUP

I have already discussed the personality traits that are likely to be present in people with mediumistic potential. However, when forming a group the most important factor is that everyone taking part are good friends. There must be complete sincerity and harmony of purpose among the sitters and each participant must be willing to give for the benefit of the whole. There is no place for self-serving egotists. Be very careful about who you invite, for it takes just one big ego to spoil it for everyone. I have met groups that have made great progress only to disband because one person let their new-found powers go to their head. So take time deciding who will sit in the group. It may be very disruptive to the energy to remove or introduce new people to the circle at a later date.

Dedication and discipline are also important factors to consider when putting together a circle. Today everyone wants instant spiritual answers and expects the fruits of spiritual endeavor to be with them from the start. These things only come with hard work and perseverance. Be prepared to sit at the very least for one year and be strict with your sitting arrangements. If you agree to start at 7:00 p.m., start exactly on time. Do not tolerate lateness. Similarly, if you agree to sit every Wednesday or alternate Wednesdays or whatever day—then do exactly that. This is some of the most important spiritual work you are likely to do in this lifetime, so think of it as making an appointment with God—and don't miss it or be late! Also remember that your spirit friends are making preparations to help your circle and they expect your dedication.

The Setting

Finding a suitable setting also requires careful planning. One of the sitters may have a spare room that you can use, though this may sometimes cause problems. For example, if the person is ill or home circumstances are disrupted for some reason then the whole group suffers. Also, if one person supplies the venue, occasionally that person may assume they "own" the group. There may also be a feeling of obligation to or from the host. Therefore, it is generally advisable to hire a space somewhere independent of the sitters and split the costs. Include a little extra in the fee to pay for refreshments, candles, flowers, etc. and ask for the weekly payment in advance so that if someone does not show up the others do not have to cover his or her share.

Check out the venue to ensure that it is quiet enough to do the meditations that will become an important part of the proceedings. Even low-level noise can be a distraction when you enter the silence of meditation. A group I ran for ten years used to meet in a wonderful fourteenth-century Tudor hotel, but eventually we had to find somewhere new when they opened a bar in one of the rooms below us. I remember us all sitting in meditation and overhearing a very drunk man below us pour his heart out to the bartender. He described in great detail his shocking sexual exploits interspersed with a volley of blue jokes. Our meditation ended in fits of hysterical laughter.

Make your setting friendly and relaxed. At first, some of the sitters may be a little nervous about what lies ahead and may have unrealistic expectations or fears about what they are likely to encounter at the meetings. They may have visions of the medium spitting green slime at the ceiling. Of course this will not be the case, but if the environment is too stark, it may magnify their fears. If people are comfortable and relaxed it will be better for the group should real physical phenomena occur.

My very first circle sat in pitch blackness and we would hear footsteps around the room. On one occasion the kettle boiled spontaneously, even though it was not plugged into the electrical outlet! Nonetheless, it was just too spooky a setting for some of the guests, and I decided to relocate the group—although it was handy having the spirit world prepare the water for tea. The eventual setting for my own circle came as a result of a *Psychic School* series I did for the BBC. At the time of writing this book, we have a room in a country house that was designed as a replica of the Alhambra Palace in Granada, Spain. It is elaborately embellished with Persian onyx, magnificent copper and bronze, and hand-cut mosaic tiles. So keep looking for a good venue—eventually the right place will find you.

There's no need for complete darkness, but subdued lighting or a red bulb is preferable for developing auric sight and mediumship. Some mediums like to work with no lighting and others prefer blue or red light. (Darkness and low red light are essential if ectoplasm is being produced, but the mental mediumship described in this book will work perfectly well in normal or low light.) So that your sitters feel at ease, it may be best to use candles at the start and move toward red light as the group feels comfortable with itself. You may want to include incense—our favorite is frankincense.

In summary: Select your members carefully. Make the group inspiring, exiting, and cheerful. Charge a fee. Find a place that has a feeling of good energy. Set goals for the funds raised to expand the sanctuary, and improve the circle environment with the addition of flowers, special candles, etc. Everyone will enjoy this expanding process and any spare funds can be used toward an end-of-year party or donated to a group-determined charity.

Who's in Charge?

If the group includes an established medium then he or she will run the proceedings and their methods may differ from what is presented here. If you do not have a medium, then you can take turns at chairing the proceedings. You may decide to have a permanent leader or alternate the role among all or a few of you. Establish a structure at the onset so that everyone knows who does what and what to expect. Get everyone involved if possible—one person may do an opening prayer or meditation, others may lead absent healing, organize the subscriptions, plan the guest speakers, or run the teaching sessions. Swap roles so that everyone feels included in this exciting journey toward spiritual insight.

In addition to your regular sitters it is of benefit to invite guest speakers, healers, psychics, and mediums to your group. If you meet a good practitioner at a special event, such as a psychic fair or spiritualist demonstration, ask them if they will address or demonstrate at your circle. Most mediums are pleased to help others to progress although they may not be able to schedule a regular session. Make sure you agree on their expenses and costs in advance and pay them discreetly soon after they arrive at your venue.

When they visit give them the option of having complete control of the evening's proceedings and allow them to teach in their own way. A trance medium may require different conditions than those described here, and individual mediums differ in their personal needs, lighting requirements, and seating arrangements. A guest medium or speaker will help you to expand your ideas and can advise on your progress.

Seating Arrangements

You need to be comfortable but not so comfortable that everyone will fall asleep during meditation. A standard high-back chair is best, as it keeps the spine, with its spiritual energy centers, straight. Remind everyone that they should use the bathroom before taking their seats, as the circle must not be interrupted once under way.

The chairs are usually arranged in a circle with the medium in a dominant position, if possible, facing the door and with a wall behind him or her. To balance the energy the medium will place a person with a powerful energy directly opposite him or her. Every circle has a number of people who generate spiritual energy and may eventually become the healers of the group. Their energy will support the others. It will become apparent who they are once the group members are able to sense auras and the balance of the energy in the room.

The medium will also sit people of high energy and/or experience on either side of him or her. This is particularly important for trance mediums, as the energy from these anchor people (including the person seated directly opposite the medium) provide the considerable energy needed during trance or materialization. With experienced people in front and on either side, the medium has a sense of protection and support.

Couples should be sat apart from one another and it is usual for members of the opposite sex to sit next to one another. This is not essential though, as not all circles have an equal number of males and females. The medium will use his or her sensitivity to the energy of the circle to make the seating decisions. These normally remain the same for each session.

A low table can be placed in the center of the group on which can be arranged pens, paper, candles, this book, and any items needed for the experiments. There should be an ample supply of water to drink between psychic links. Water provides spiritual energy (known as *chi* or *prana*) and cleanses the practitioners vibrations of any conditions, such as memories of the spirit's terminal illness, that are sensed during the spirit communications.

Sitting

So long as it is comfortable for you, it is best to sit upright but relaxed. If the spine is straight then the spiritual energies that we use in mediation and mediumship can travel freely up and down the spinal column. If you slump, you will not be fully alert and may even fall to sleep, which will be very annoying to the serious students. Yoga meditation encourages students to sit on the front edge of the seat without leaning against the chair back. The hands are then rested on your knees, palm down. The ideal chair-sitting posture has the ear, shoulder, and hip in alignment as viewed from the side.

Sit how you feel most comfortable, either with your hands in the yoga position described above or with your back against the chair and your hands on your lap. Some people like to put their hands in a symbolic hand position called a *mudra*. The most commonly known one is the **O** shape, symbolizing the unity of all things. You sit with your palms facing up and forefingers touching thumbs, creating the circle of life. Keep your feet flat on the ground. Some mediums believe that crossing your legs and arms blocks the flow of your spiritual energy.

Working on Your Own
Most of the experiments and techniques I am going to show you require participants, so I will explain the techniques with the circle setting as the default. However, it is certainly possible to practice many of these experiments with open-minded friends and family, and I hope you will practice both within a group and on your own. You will be able to adapt these techniques easily to suit your needs. Nonetheless, few mediums develop their gifts completely outside of a circle setting as the collective energy provides the conditions necessary for accelerating the development of the spiritual powers. It is therefore advisable to join or form a circle if you can.

THE CIRCLE'S FORMAT

Even the most spiritual groups need a structure. Like a good story, the circle's structure should have a clear beginning, middle, and end. In this case, we have an opening that includes mediation and attunement, an experimental session in the middle, and a closing period to bring you back into normal awareness.

Every member of the group should have a notebook and pen with them to keep a record of any spirit messages given by them and to them and also to note any information received during meditation. My groups usually last about two hours, including a bit of chitchat afterward. I will now explain the stages in detail.

Opening the Circle

1. **Incantation.** Some mediums like to open their circles with a prayer. I prefer a positive statement, as people have a different understanding of what we mean by the word "God." It could be argued that if God lies within us, then it is perhaps unnecessary to externalize our concept of God by means of prayer. Nonetheless, a positive affirmation makes a good starting point for the session and focuses everyone's attention. I usually say something like: "We ask that a bridge of light be built between the two worlds. May our work be protected and blessed by the divine power in a spirit of love and compassion. The circle is now open." You can change the words to suit your own beliefs, but I would suggest you keep it short.

2. **Breathing.** If we allow the breath to become calm, the inner world will also become calm. A few minutes quieting the breath will prepare the group for meditation and help them to let go of the tension of the day. I usually say: "Sitting comfortably, listening to my voice, you may feel the pressures of the day falling away. You may want to relax very deeply and you are able to let go of all stress. Deeply relax, more and more, and be aware of how good you are starting to feel. You are able to leave your worries behind because this is *your* time to enjoy *your* right to deep inner peace. Notice how your body is becoming more and more at ease. You are probably already feeling how the breath is calming down. So it is easy now to take a deep breath in . . . and as you breath out, think to yourself: *relax*. Maybe you want to do this a few times?"

3. **Meditation.** The circle is now ready to move into meditation. Later I will explain methods of meditation in more detail and explain why we open the spiritual centers known as the charkas.

   For the first sessions you will work with the full chakra meditation, which I will describe in detail later in the book. The method establishes a spiritual routine to enable you to open your aura and increase your spiritual sensitivity. Once this routine becomes familiar to the group, you can use a shortened version of the method or just ask the group to move into meditation using the chakra technique. At first you may want to read the full meditation aloud. The full meditation is now available on CD from my website at www.psychics.co.uk

The meditation is usually done in silence so that people can attune themselves with their spirit helpers. In the early stages, the meditation lasts only a few minutes and is increased as the aspirants learn to sit. I prefer a long period of meditation, as it is so good to escape the banal world and return to the blissful peace that lies within. Unfortunately not everyone is a good meditator and some may fidget, sigh, or sleep through meditation. Use your own judgment regarding timing based upon your observation of the members.

You may conclude the meditation by ringing a small bell and saying something like: "Soon it will be time to end the meditation. In your own time please return to normal awareness."

4. **Impressions.** At first, some of the group may find meditation uncomfortable and have unusual thoughts and sensations. This is natural and is usually a result of their day-to-day tensions and stress. Relaxing deeply makes us aware of our tensions and also of how hectic our normal thinking is. Reassure them that stress and an overactive mind will be replaced by comfort and inner peace once they become accustomed to the art of meditation.

I sometimes like to encourage members of the circle to talk about their experiences in meditation. Some of the sitters will experience inner-light, states of deep relaxation and feelings of great calm and peace. Often the sitters will have visions and see fantastic dreamlike imagery. In traditional forms of meditation these impressions are dismissed as a distraction from the spiritual goal of meditation, which eventually results in enlightenment. However, for the development of clairvoyance they can prove useful. For example, you may see a spirit guide, friends from the afterlife, or be given symbols that relate to your own experiences or the experiences of others sitting in the group.

The things you see, hear, and feel in your meditation are very often the start of clairvoyant insight. Many times sitters will see similar guide figures or symbols, and experience settings that are similar to one another. A fascinating telepathic bonding occurs in a circle that may yield many useful insights.

Later I will explain how to target your mediations and will suggest some experiments you can try to increase this spiritual bonding. I will also explain how to 'sit for spirit' – that is specifically meditate to allow the spirit people to come close prior to giving a reading. Nonetheless, do not get too distracted by the impressions and clairvoyance that occurs in meditation. We meditate so that we can link to the spiritual part of ourselves. It prepares us for the work ahead and gives us an opportunity to charge ourselves with spiritual energy. Enjoy this experience.

Psychic and Mediumistic Experimentation

The middle part of the circle session is used to practice your psychic and mediumistic skills. I will be describing these step by step and in detail throughout this book. You will start with psychometry (reading vibrations from an object), then develop your gift through linking to a person's aura (the spiritual vibration of an individual that is sometimes seen as light), and eventually learn to link to the vibrations of the spirit world. My method is a gradual process that requires patience and perseverance but will result in solid and evidential mediumship.

Although it is traditional to sit in a circle while conducting the experiments, you may sometimes vary the routine. Try the experiments in a standing position, sometimes work in pairs sitting in front of one another, or move the chairs to form a block with one of you standing and demonstrating in front of the group.

The time required for this stage of development will vary for the individuals working in the group. If some advance quickly, then it is their duty to help others up the ladder to full consciousness. You are a spiritual team and it is important that the group leader ensures that everyone gets a turn during the session if possible. Do not just concentrate on the best pupils. Everyone sitting is giving of his or her time and spiritual energy, so it is only fair that everyone have a try. Do not underestimate how important it is for the participants to get even a small detail right during the session—they will be buzzing with excitement at having gotten something correct.

Every successful verification of your psychic and mediumistic readings is another step toward high-quality practice. Material things come and go but spiritual qualities come and grow! Once you become a medium it is like swimming or riding a bike—you never forget it.

Closing the Circle

1. **Call to order.** Most of the time it will be easy for the evening's circle leader to remind everyone that the circle needs to close. However, if you have split the members into pairs you will find that everyone will be completely immersed in their readings and the rooms buzzing with talk. They will probably try to ignore you when you call time. It is therefore important to remind people in advance and say: "In a few minutes we will be finishing, so please start completing your reading now." Then when it is actually time to close the circle you can be firm and make everyone stop together.

2. **Absent healing.** When you have finished practicing, the spiritual energy that has been generated can be used for absent healing. Everyone closes their eyes and one member of the circle talks the others through a visualization. Each person in turn names those people they would like healing to be sent to, each time with the speaker talking the group through the visualization.

3. **Closing the aura.** The evening's group leader talks the group through the closing of the aura and charkas. Allow the aura to gradually return to its normal rate of vibration and the mind to come back to everyday awareness. It is important that all circle members pay strict attention to this particularly if driving home.

4. **Refreshments.** This is the time for chitchat. You'll have lots to talk about after the circle and as a result, many of the participants are likely to become some of your closest friends.

AN EXPERIMENT TO TRY
Write a Spiritual Diary

Keeping a spiritual diary can be a very useful tool not only during your development in circle but throughout your life. It will help you to chart your progress and encourage you by keeping tabs on how well you are doing. Soon we will be trying a number of psychic experiments, so it is particularly helpful to keep notes about what you say and have a record of messages that you have been given or that you give during the sessions. You can buy a quality notebook for this purpose, as this is valuable work you are doing and your notes will be something that you may want to look at in years to come. In your spiritual diary you could include:

Clairvoyance: Keep note of the hits that you get right when you work with others in the circle or with friends. For example if you give a particularly good reading, keep a note of the most important or unusual points you got right about the sitter or the spirit communicator such as the names, descriptions of the spirit's personality, life history and so on. This will encourage you to keep working by giving you proof of how capable you are of being right.

Messages to you: Note any messages and evidence that others give you during circle or during private consultations with other mediums. During the developing stages of your mediumship you are likely to get many very important messages that will guide your long-term spiritual progress. Some of these may become relevant in years to come.

Your experiences: Write about your past and present spiritual experiences, such as visits to haunted houses or spontaneous experiences you may have. Try to remember details such as dates and ways of confirming the happenings. This will help to reinforce your memory of the experiences and your ability to provide the facts should you need to support your arguments for the existence of ESP.

Psychic dreams: Dreams will help you to access your intuitive skills and put you in touch with your higher self. During your psychic development you will go through many inner changes and will probably have many vivid dreams. Use your spiritual diary to record and work with your dreams.

Experiments: You can also use your spiritual diary to make a record of your psychic experiments such as predictions, psychic art, and advance clairvoyance experiments.

Inspiration: Write down any quotes and affirmations that inspire you. Also, do some of your own creative writing. You may feel very creative immediately after a period of meditation or sitting and it is useful to write down your insights before they fade..

3 QUICK WAYS TO GET STARTED

"All our interior world is reality—and that perhaps more so than our apparent world."
—**Marc Chagall**

Mental mediumship is an inner experience. Spirit communicators use telepathy to interact with our thoughts and to give us information about the continuation of life and the survival of the personality after physical death. Our eventual goal is to discover how to unlock mediumistic potential, but in order to do this you first need to train your psychic skills. Through ESP you can discover things about members on the circle and people you meet in general. I will show you how to do this by employing techniques such as psychometry, aura reading, and psychic sensing. As a prelude to this, I am going to show you a few simple and fun experiments that will quickly get you started. When used in the context of a group, the following methods will inspire initial confidence and, because they involve the familiar skills of drawing and coloring, are not intimidating to the beginner. You will need paper, inks, water, brushes, a ruler, a compass, and colored pencils for the experiments that follow.

SUBCONSCIOUS ESP

In a moment I am going to ask you to make a random shape on paper using black ink and water. You will look for pictures and images in the blot of ink and interpret these as symbols. But first I need to explain how the subconscious mind is engaged in ESP and why this inkblot technique is so effective.

When we work as a psychic or medium, information appears to come to us from "out of nowhere" but in reality it is the subconscious mind working behind the scenes that is giving us this information. Just like ideas that arise of themselves, so too information from the sixth sense just pops into our heads. Sometimes this comes via our own subconscious ESP and later, when mediumship develops, it comes from the spirit people. In both instances the subconscious mind plays a very active role.

In my other books I have called this process *psychic intuition*. It is this that gives us those initial psychic experiences of hunches, gut feelings, and dream premonitions. Some of the information we get in this way comes from ourselves, but there is also an element that comes through spontaneous extrasensory perception. I intend to make you aware of this faculty and will show you how to tap into it.

Just about everyone, at some time, has had a hunch that proves to be true. When you reflect upon how you knew the things you knew there is often no logical explanation other than there was some clairvoyant influence involved. Spontaneous psychic hunches are a wonderful starting point remain a hit-and-miss affair and are outside of our conscious control. If we are to work as psychics or mediums we need to develop a greater degree of control and know how to switch the gift on and off. Stimulating the subconscious helps us to improve and trigger these impromptu hunches.

PROJECTING THE PSYCHIC INTUITION

When you were a child you probably gazed at white cumulus clouds drifting in the blue sky and noticed how they formed into fantastic shapes of faces, animals, and spectacular landscapes. These changing images reflect what is happening in your own subconscious mind. Similarly, the pictures seen in a fire's embers, the patterns in sand, a rock formation, the gnarled bark of a tree, or the tasseomancer's tea leaves reveal your hidden psychological processes. The psychologist Carl Jung called these spontaneous expressions of the subconscious the active imagination. It is the threshold between our everyday awareness and the dreamlike world of the subconscious.

The Jungian psychoanalyst Hermann Rorschach realized that the mind's ability to project visual images could be used to discover what was happening in the minds of people undergoing psychiatric therapy. While playing a children's game called blotto, in which children look for pictures in inkblots, it struck him that what the children were seeing in the shapes revealed a great deal about their psychological condition. From this simple game he devised the Rorschach test, which today is considered one of the best psychodiagnostic procedures and an indispensable tool of psychiatry. The test involves the patient describing the images he or she sees in specially designed inkblots. From the patient's description the psychoanalyst gains insight to what is happening in the patient's subconscious mind.

Visually projected active imagination is not only a link to your own inner processes but psychics believe it also links you to your psychic intuition. For centuries psychics have interpreted the pictures they see in tea leaves, hot coals, smoke shapes, sand patterns, and even sacrificial entrails as symbols that represent the conditions surrounding anyone who has inquired of the oracle. (The word oracle comes from the Latin *orare* meaning to speak or pray. An oracle can be a person who is the mouthpiece for prophecy or a tool used to make a prophecy or give an insight into the course of the future.)

For our experiment we are going to use the mind's ability to project pictures onto a random shape to give a reading to a volunteer. The objective of this exercise is to demonstrate how the images emerging from the subconscious contain psychic content that is relevant to the person receiving the reading. The inkblot will become a mirror to your psychic intuition.

Psychic Inkblot Experiment

You can use any number of things to create your random pattern: tea leaves, clouds, or the patterns formed in a crumpled sheet of paper are a few examples. I have had fun sometimes reading the images I see in dirty dishes after a dinner party and, of course, it is a good excuse for not washing them right away. Any random pattern can be used to give this sort of reading, but in this instance we are going to make an inkblot. You can make the blots in advance of the session or they can be made at the time of the reading. I also have designed a set of "intuition cards," which feature ready-made inkblots and other experiments (details available on my website).

Step 1. You will need white paper, black ink, an artist's paintbrush, and water. This experiment can be messy so use plenty of old newspapers to protect your table and/or carpets. Divide everyone into pairs. One person will read and the other will be read.

Step 2. Using a paintbrush, put some drops of water and drops of black ink onto a sheet of paper. Now fold the paper in half so that the water and ink merge to form shapes and tones in a symmetrical pattern—just as you may have done in school to create "butterflies." Allow it a few minutes to dry.

Step 3. Relax as you look at the inkblot. Let your imagination discover pictures in the shapes. It is likely that the first things you will notice in the swirls of ink are faces and figures. Ask yourself what emotions these faces symbolize: Are they happy, sad, perplexed, angry, contemplative, or whatever? The mood expressed by the face may symbolize how the sitter has been feeling. Describe what you see to your recipient and discuss it if it relates to the way he or she has been feeling recently.

Step 4: Once you are accustomed to seeing pictures, you will eventually notice more subtle images. Look not only in the black areas but in the white areas too. See what pictures are formed there—much like a negative image. Look at the overall shape, but if you look closely you will also see pictures in the edges of the shapes and in the small details of the inkblot. The images that are most important are the ones you feel most drawn too, for it is your psychic intuition that is bringing your attention to them.

Step 5: Describe the images you see and what they mean to you. Explain what you believe this is saying about the person sitting in front of you. Say what you feel without trying to change it or over-rationalize. The pictures are symbols, so explain what you feel they represent. If you know a little about the meanings of dream symbols you can apply some of this knowledge. For example, if you see a bird you could interpret this as the sitter's desire to escape a problem, or perhaps it represents a desire to attain higher knowledge or freedom. A bird flying away from the nest may indicate someone leaving home or taking the plunge in a new enterprise. Or maybe the image is literal: The sitter may keep birds! Symbols are fluid things and there is no set interpretation. Use your intuition rather than logic to discover and explain what is meaningful to the sitter.

Step 6: Work with the images to see if there are other hidden meanings. Help the sitter to understand what issues are important and give some clear and sensible advice about how they can make the best of things. Perhaps you can gain insight into material you could not possibly know, such as stories from the sitter's childhood, his or her interests, hopes, and failures in life, and so on. Ask if the sitter can verify the information now coming from your psychic insights.

Step 7: When you have finished, ask the sitter how he or she felt about the reading and if the symbols meant anything different to him or her. The sitter may want to talk about some of the problems you identified, and you may want to give a little advice. Empower the sitter to deal with the issues rather than make predictions.

Step 8. Now swap roles and try the experiment again.

Studying the projected imagery that arises from the unconscious is a quick way of accessing your latent powers. Similar psychic aids include sand reading, in which the random patterns found in a tray of sand are interpreted, and scrying techniques such gazing into a crystal ball, mirror, hearth fire, bowl of water, or black ink. Each of these psychic tools act as a focus for the attention while the intuitive mind unfolds.

PSYCHIC ART

Research has shown that imaginative, creative people—particularly artists—core better in ESP tests than analytic thinkers. Some of my first psychic insights came while I was painting in oils. I was inspired by the surrealist painter Max Ernst, who used the decalcomania technique, which involved putting pigment on the canvas, laying sheets of paper or glass on top, and removing them quickly. Just as we did with our inkblots, Ernst would recognize images in the paint's shapes and added color, light, and shadows to emphasize what he could see, thus making the images obvious to the viewer. My favorite is his painting called *The Eye of Silence* (1943–44, Milred Lane Kemper Museum, Washington University Gallery, St Louis), which includes bizarre images reminiscent of those we see in the inkblot experiment.

As with the work of many surrealist painters, Ernst's pictures have a threatening theme but nonetheless is of interest to anyone studying the projected imagination methods I have described. It is interesting to note also that many surrealists were influenced by Spiritualism. In particular, the surrealists were interested in automatic drawing and writing and hailed the French psychic Helen Smith as the "muse of automatic writing." Personally I find some of her communications from Martians a little suspect, but I can see how this interested the surrealists. Surrealists rejected Spiritualism in its manifestos but nonetheless adopted its methods. For example, the surrealist Robert Desnos (1900–45) performed séances for poetic purposes but made no claims to the truth of their revelations.

During it's hey day Spiritualism saw some incredible psychic artists at work. One of the most famous was the Scottish medium David Duguid (1832–1907,) who could produce oil paintings of landscapes in total darkness, at an amazing speed, and independently of his hands. The psychical investigator Frank Podmore witnessed these incredible feats of psychic mediumship—called precipitation—so that there would be no opportunity to cheat. Also of note are the mediums Allan B. Campbell (1833–1919) and

Charles Campbell (born Charles Shourds) from Lily Dale near New York. More widely known as the Campbell brothers, they precipitated spirit-inspired pastel and oil portraits, including an interesting rendition of Allan Campbell's spirit guide, Azur.

The Bang sisters, whose pictures manifest in front of an audience, accomplished some of the most astonishing precipitation of art. In one famous demonstration in August 1911, at the Chesterfield Spiritualist Camp in Indiana, they precipitated a painting of a young girl. Gradually a picture the background appeared, followed by the face of a young girl with her eyes closed. Then the eyes opened and the picture was complete. A non-Spiritualist dignitary named Mr. Alfords claimed the portrait was the exact likeness of his "dead" daughter, Audrey.

If you have artistic talent, the spirit people will encourage you to use it in your mediumistic work. Working with images also connects the medium to the unconscious, and color, light, natural form, and geometry appeal to our spiritual nature. For this next experiment you will need paper and colored pencils. You do not need drawing skills, as this can be accomplished by anyone.

Auragraph Experiment

Auragraphs are drawings or paintings produced by psychics and mediums to depict the aura. One of the first exponents of this technique was the medium Harold Sharp, who worked under the influence of his Chinese spirit guide. This enabled him to design an artistic diagram of the human aura, which is called an auragraph.

Most auragraphs are produced as a circle to represent the wholeness of the self. Sharp produced colored circles with pictures in them, but I also have seen mediums produce auragraphs in other ways, including working with shapes such as a butterfly, with one side representing the inner life and the other the outer life. I have also seen auragraphs in the shape of a peacock feather or as a pictorial mind map that starts from a single point and weaves into lines and tangents and eventually fills the page with written comments and imagery as the reading progresses. Auragraphs can be very personal and later you may devise your own way of working.

Auragraphs usually show other information that is intuitively received by way of the aura, such as the story of a person's life, their spiritual condition, their way forward, and so on. Sometimes auragraphs are a direct representation of the aura as it appears around the body with an explanation about what the various colors say about the recipient. Auragraphs can also be drawn in an abstract way and will usually include symbolism, particularly the symbolism associated with color.

For this next experiment we are going to produce a simple auragraph in the shape of a mandala, but you may experiment with whatever style or drawing method you like. The form is not as important as the content, which will include psychic information about the person being given the reading.

The word *mandala* comes from Sanskrit for "magic circle." Mandalas are sacred, geometric designs used for meditation purposes. The simplest kind of mandala is a circle but, particularly in Tibetan Buddhism, they are usually intricate drawings in paint or sand with a series of concentric circles or squares radiating from a central point. For Tibetan Buddhists the mandala is a blueprint by which a person meditating can realize specific spiritual states represented by its geometry and symbolism.

The psychologist Carl Jung noticed that mandala images often emerged in dreams and paintings during analysis of his patients. His research led him to the conclusion that mandalas are an archetypal expression of the self and wholeness. Jung would ask his patients to draw mandalas and discovered that they were very powerful tools that could be used to reveal the processes happening in the unconscious. He found that drawing mandalas was also very therapeutic and stimulated a sense of inner harmony in the artist.

We will use the geometry of a mandala for our auragraph. Other examples of how to do auragraphs are described in my book *The Psychic Workbook*.

Step 1. The group leader pairs everyone; one person will be the reader and draw the auragraph and the other will be the sitter and receive the messages.

Step 2. With a compass and ruler the reader draws a large circle and divides it through the center into four equal segments, so it looks like a compass. The top two segments represent the higher self and the spiritual aspirations of the sitter. The bottom two segments represent the worldly concerns of the sitter. (This shape also promotes harmony, as it corresponds with Carl Jung's theory of "fourfoldness," which in mandalas is often represented by a perfect geometrical grouping of four, a square, or the quartering of a circle.)

Step 3. The human brain has two hemispheres that perform different psychological specializations and this is represented in the auragraph mandala. The two segments on the left of the circle represent all that is logical and rational. On this side of the circle you will give information about things that the sitter is conscious.

The remaining segments on the right represent the sitter's intuitive nature, his or her feelings and creative nature. This side also shows issues that the recipient/sitter is not consciously aware of. The very center of the circle represents the most powerful driving forces and aspirations that are presently with the person receiving the reading. This division of spiritual at the top, worldly below, rational on the left, and intuitive on the right provides a simple framework to build your visual representation of the sitter's spiritual and psychological situation.

Step 4. If you find my framework a little complicated just work in any way you feel best. As I have said, content is more important than form. As you interpret the drawing, tell your sitter what you are sensing and discuss it. Try not to feed back things the sitter has told you but trust your intuition to give you the insight you need.

Step 5. As you sense information about the person sitting in front of you, add color patterns and pictures into the appropriate areas of the auragraph. For example, if you feel the person has high spiritual ideals you may add the color violet to the segments at the top. If you feel that this is something that is just beginning to flow, you want to add patterns in swirl of violet tones here to show a flow of energy. Or you may have a feeling that you want to add red to the shape. If you look up red in the aura section, you will read that if this color is found in the body aura, it shows a dynamic—possibly angry—person. However, red added to the spiritual areas of the aura high above the head can show spiritual power, such as mediumship. If it was anger you sensed, then you would probably want to add red tones to the one of lower segments, perhaps on the bottom right, as here is represented the root of the emotions. If the red comes to you as a spiritual color, then you would add it to one or both of the top segments: on the left to show mediumship that the sitter is aware of, and on the right to indicate mediumship that is developing.

Step 6. Draw patterns with your colored pencils to represent the nature of the energy itself. For example, discordant or jarring shapes may indicate conflicts, whereas flowing lines and circles may show harmony. Squares suggest a standstill, which may mean that the sitter's potential is either not being used or is stagnating. Using a combination of patterns and shapes will give you many ways to represent how you feel about the sitter's energy. At this point in your development we do not expect you to be able to sense or see the aura, but your intuition will, nonetheless, tell you a great deal about the person before you.

Step 7. Also add simple doodles and pictures to the drawing. As with the inkblot experiments, these images may represent things about the person's situation or character. Draw the images and interpret them. To jog the sitter's memory later you can also add a few key words that explain the most important things you have said. Scribbling down your flow of thoughts and using lots of colors distracts your conscious mind and allows you to naturally express your psychic side.

At first your auragraphs may be a little messy, but with practice they can become decorative artworks that have value in their own right. Auragraphs are like large colored doodles that you produce as the psychic intuition flows. They are visual recordings of the readings that will be of value to the recipients.

Step 8. Discuss any other issues that may not have been spoken about while the reading was taking place and when you have finished reverse roles.

PSYCHIC PORTRAITURE

Some mediums who are competent artists in their own right are able to sketch the faces of communicating spirits to give proof of the survival of death. My wife, Jane, and I were fortunate to have a number of consultations with one of the United Kingdom's most famous psychic artists, Coral Polge, who has produced some astonishing drawings of spirit communicators. When compared to photographs of the deceased it is clear that her drawings show details that are very specific to the communicating spirit. In addition to a striking likeness, Coral's drawings would include details such as moles, broken noses, and scars, and often is an exact replication of an existing photo. One of Jane's most treasured pictures is a drawing Coral made of John Stokes, the husband of the medium Doris Stokes, and who has now passed into spirit. John gave Jane away at our wedding.

When working in a public forum, psychic artists often like to work with another medium who will tune in to the spirit communicator and give proof while the psychic artist gets on with drawing the portrait. The combined information from both mediums can provide wonderful evidence of survival as well a lovely drawing for the sitter to take home as a memento. Sometimes psychic artists work in trance and the spirit controls their arms as the drawings are produced.

If there is a particularly gifted artist in my circle I encourage him or her to draw as he or she links to spirit. The illustrator of this book, Steinar Lund, is currently learning to do this and occasionally has produced accurate representations of people known to our sitters. It is important, however, to also provide lots of mediumistic evidence to accompany the drawings to ensure that recipients are not just making the face fit. Steinar is a good artist and provides mental mediumship as he draws the portraits, so it is easy to immediately recognize the person. I have seen quite the opposite in demonstrations by some psychic artists whose work borders on the hilarious. For example, Jane and I, together with our young daughter, Danielle (about 6 years old at the time), watched what we considered to be a very funny demonstration of psychic art. The medium clearly could not draw and produced monstrous portraits of "loved ones" that to us resembled characters from horror movies. It was embarrassing holding back the giggles, but to our utter astonishment someone in the audience actually accepted one as their grandfather. "Her granddad looks like Freddie Kruger from *Nightmare on Elm Street*," piped up Danielle.

ADVANCE AND REMOTE CLAIRVOYANCE

To get started with psychic portraiture I encourage students to do the drawings in advance of coming to the circle. They are also requested to write down any information they believe comes from the spirit communicator. If we have a guest, I ask them to produce something specifically for them. At the next meeting, they read out their notes and show the portrait. In most instances what is shown and said is accepted by the recipient. This is a form of advance clairvoyance.

Many people find it hard to believe that it is possible for a medium to pick up information about someone they are not sitting with or have never met, but this is exactly what happens in many forms of reading. For example, on my website I have sometimes given mediumistic readings by email. All I have to go by is a few simple questions, so I have to rely entirely on remote clairvoyance, that is, clairvoyance done with the sitter absent. One example that comes to mind was for Stojanka, a woman from the former Yugoslavia who asked by email a series of very specific questions about the person in the spirit with whom she wished to communicate. She set what I initially thought was an impossible task, but which proved to be a good example of how very detailed mediumship can work even when the sitter isn't present:

Stojanka asked, "What is the secret code that I told to my father?" In reply I gave her the color red and the postal code and number (six numbers) of her father's army garrison. The secret code between the father and daughter was the same number I had quoted together with the words *red fox*. I didn't get the fox part, but taken with the other correct answers, such as my description of her father's unusual car—an Opel Olympia—and how her sister died in the snow, I believe that the evidence points to a proof of life after death. The intriguing thing about this example is that all this came via email and without me ever meeting, seeing, or talking to Stojanka. (I did meet her sometime later when she flew to the U.K. for a reading.)

Through remote clairvoyance it is also possible to provide information for someone whom the medium may never meet through a proxy who receives it on behalf of the absent friend.

Just as it is possible to make a spirit communication remotely, it is also possible to write down a reading for someone in advance of meeting them. Try the following experiment in advance clairvoyance.

Advance Clairvoyance Experiment

Step 1. If the circle leader has arranged to have a guest for the following week, an announcement should be made to that effect, but the leader should be careful not to give away any information about the mystery person. Everyone who is coming to the next meeting will write notes or draw pictures in their spiritual diaries to bring with them.

Step 2. At home the circle members meditate at a convenient time and write any impressions they receive about the guest into their spiritual diaries. If there is no guest for the upcoming week, then they write information that may relate to other members of the circle and to their family and friends. Messages can be passed on and confirmed or denied in future weeks.

Step 3. At the next meeting, after the meditation session, each person takes a turn to read aloud his or her notes. The guest will confirm or negate any facts being given. If while reading out their notes the circle member feels he or she would like to give more information, they can, with the permission of the group leader, give a short psychic or mediumistic reading at this time.

Advance clairvoyance is a good way to get everyone in the circle working. At the early stages of development it feels much easier to write something down at home than to make a link while everyone is watching you. Yet although it is a less intimidating way to work, advance clairvoyance is, in fact, one of the purest forms of mediumship you can achieve. It is not influenced by body language, facial expressions, or appearances. There is no opportunity to inadvertently feed back information that has already slipped out, and there is no chance of mind reading or picking up information from the person's aura. If information has been correctly given about a spirit person by advance clairvoyance there is only one way the medium could have gotten it—and that is straight from the spirit communicator.

4 SENSING VIBRATIONS AND PSYCHOMETRY

"On such things as matter we have all been wrong, what we have called matter is energy, whose vibration has been so lowered as to be perceptible to the senses. There is no matter."
—Alfred Einstein

It is said that the birds never sing at the former Nazi extermination camps of Belsen, Dachau, and Auschwitz. God's creatures know that these places "smell of death" and are filled with the dark vibrations of the past. Intuitively knowing that a place is dangerous has survival value. This instinct has been passed on to us by our archaic ancestors. Not only can we sense fear from bad places but we are also aware of benign and helpful vibrations. When we enter a place of worship there is a feeling of holiness from the centuries of worship that is imprinted into the structure of the building. Similarly the vibrations at an amusement park will buzz with excitement and a theater will be infused with the emotional energy left behind by audiences. The impressions we get are more than what our senses tell us: there is something "in the air."

This feeling of the vibration of a place, which we commonly refer to as having good or bad "vibes," becomes particularly sharp when we buy property. We don't just choose a place because of price, room sizes, and location. It has to "feel right." It has to "feel like home." You may have noticed that some places have a bad atmosphere and others feel welcoming. One of my daughters works in real estate and says that many house purchasers will ask if any of the previous occupants were divorced or if anyone ever died in the house. A great many people are concerned by the vibrations that are left by former occupants and ask whether there is a history of violence, murder, or crime connected to the property. Houses with a bad vibe or a dark history just don't sell.

Why is it that certain places have a feeling of foreboding? Mediums and psychics believe that thought travels outside of our body and is absorbed into the environment. This would account for why some places have a definite atmosphere. A psychically sensitive person may become aware of these vibrations and respond to the memories that are imprinted onto the area's energy field. For example, if a terrible event such as a murder happened, then they may "see" that event in their mind's eye. And if they are very sensitive they may see the event with their physical eyes as well. Most ghost sightings are a result of a psychically sensitive person responding to the vibrations "recorded" in the environment, which they see as an apparition. This, of course, differs from the self-aware spirit of someone who is living a new life and makes themselves known to us.

Places may also retain the residue energy of historic events and the thoughts and feeling of people who once lived there. I have received many letters and emails through my newspaper columns from people who have had very powerful experiences in which they momentarily have been transported back in time and "seen" events from history happening around them. I have posted some of these extraordinary accounts on my websites. Perhaps these people have experienced the historic recordings I have been writing about or it may be that they encountered a brief time slip and directly experienced these past events. If our consciousness is not subject to the constraints of time, then it follows that these people could indeed be seeing directly into history. Skeptics argue that it is just fantasy, but in many instances the person is able to recall facts that were completely unknown to them at the time.

Many of the leading archaeologists, such as Heinrich Schliemann and Arthur Evans, have been attuned to the idea that places and relics may retain memories of the past. Major historic discoveries are often found, not through systematic excavation, but because of a hunch. Something leads the seeker to dig in a particular place where great treasures are unearthed. For example, Bligh Bond recounts in his book, *The Gate of Remembrance,* how the Edgar Chapel in the abbey of Glastonbury in Somerset, England, was discovered using clairvoyance. Similarly, a number of archaeologists have used psychics in their digs with considerable success. Dr. Norman Emerson of the University of Toronto reported being assisted in his digs by a businessman named George McMullen, who had a sharp talent for locating ruins and reconstructing their associated history.

Objects that also retain the energy of the past can be intuitively accessed using clairvoyance. To demonstrate this, BBC Television asked me to prove that memories of the past can be embedded into objects or locations. With experts on hand to verify my findings, I was to tell the history of three mystery items when taken to their locations by car. My primary task was to identify three historical characters using artifacts from southern England's past. To make it harder, I had to remain blindfolded for the entire journey, ensuring that the locations were as much a mystery as the items themselves.

The first artifact was an oval jewel set in gold. Unbeknownst to me it was part of an aestel commissioned by King Alfred and held in the Salisbury Museum. It would have held an ivory pointer and was used by clergymen to follow words on a manuscript, particularly a bible. I identified the object as a pointer and correctly picked up on the age of the jewel and the male connection. The second location was an old library where I was handed a model of a head. I correctly stated that it was the death mask of an unrepentant murderer who was hanged.

The most exciting challenge came when my blindfold was removed in an unremarkable room in a Victorian country house. I was handed me a violin. Immediately I felt that this violin had not been played by a skilled musician. I correctly stated that the instrument was played for fun from childhood and that it was part of a set that included a cello. I identified the owner as an author, and came up with several possible names, including Thomas Hardy. The curator was astonished. The violin indeed had been owned by Dorset-based author Thomas Hardy in the late 1800s. Hardy was taught to play by his father and he played the instrument for fun at local dances. It is now on display at Max Gate, Hardy's home near Dorchester.

WHAT IS PSYCHOMETRY?

Reading the vibrations from an object is called psychometry. The word comes from the Greek *psyche* (soul) and *metron* (measure), and literally means "measuring of the soul." The term was coined in the mid-nineteenth century by Joseph Rodes Buchanan, an American professor of physiology from the Eclectic Medical Institute, in Covington, Kentucky. Buchanan noticed that some of his students could distinguish different chemicals when they are wrapped in thick brown paper and discovered that some of these "sensitives" could also describe, from unopened letters, the contents and character of the writer.

Psychometry is used in psychic archaeology and psychic criminology, and is an important part of Spiritualist training for developing mediumship. In the U.K. the law states that psychometry must only be used as a training aid, as to hold an object while purporting to be making a link to the spirit world is an infringement of the provisions of the Fraudulent Mediums Act of 1951. It is argued that the information obtained from psychometry is not a spirit link if it is being obtained from an object. No tools or aids such as tarot cards, crystal balls, and so on are required to make contact with the spirit world and must not be used as part of a mediumistic reading. It is therefore necessary to put the object down when moving from a psychometry reading to a mediumistic one.

DEVELOPING THE SKILL OF PSYCHOMETRY

For an accomplished medium the vibration emanating from a personal object held at the start of a sitting can act as a stepping stone that links them with the vibrations of communicators from the spirit world. The novice can also use psychometry as the foundation for their clairvoyance, which may eventually grow into a mediumistic gift. Grounding in psychometry trains the intuition to sense qualities of the owner's character from an object. This same intuitive skill can eventually be developed into the ability to sense the personality and thoughts of a spirit communicator.

If you are running a group then you will probably practice psychometry every week. At the start it will help you and the other group members to develop your innate psychic skills. In a developed circle it will serve as a useful warm-up before beginning mediumship. Do not undervalue the importance of psychometry or get frustrated because you want to dive straight into mediumship. Develop extremely accurate psychometry and your mediumship is likely to become just as accurate.

Basic Psychometry Experiment

When people come to the circle I ask them all to put at least one object into a bag as they enter. These can be "read" during the evening. It is important that nobody else in the room sees the objects being put into the bag or be given clues to identify its owner.

Some psychics claim that metal and stone objects are best for psychometry, as they easily retain the vibrations. I consider this hearsay, as I have not noticed any difference. An object that has been worn is particularly useful because it has been in direct contact with the person to be read. Similarly, older objects are more suitable than brand-new ones that have not had much time to absorb vibrations. It is also important to know the history of the object in case the psychometrist gives information about multiple owners of the item. It is best if the object to be read has had only one owner.

The practitioners may add their own items to the bag and may also bring along objects lent to them by friends and family. It is advisable to record the session if the subject of the reading is absent, and then asking him or her to write some comments that can be read out the next time. Being correct using this remote form of psychometry can be very encouraging for the readers and is validation of the accuracy of their gift—particularly if the recipient was initially skeptical. However, for the first sessions, keep to just objects from the sitters in the room, as it is good in the first stages to get an immediate response so that you can instantly see how well you are doing and feel your confidence increase.

I encourage my sitters to include personal items such as keys, jewelry, and watches, but also to include letters, loaned objects, and something with an unusual history. If the history and people associated with the objects are interesting then the resulting clairvoyance for that session is likely to be intriguing. If any of the group has access to historic artifacts or implements used in a crime, include these also.

Psychometry is a comparatively easy psychic skill to learn and you may find that you get quick and accurate information right from the start.

Objectives of the psychometry session: The thoughts we project into the world are absorbed by objects we have owned for a long period of time. It is the objective of this session to "replay" these recordings. In particular, we are interested in discovering information about the owner(s) of the objects we hold. We hope to build up an extensive character profile and include information about their personality and their life.

Step 1. The leader of the group selects a person from the circle to do the first psychometry reading. The history of the object should be unknown to the reader but known by someone in the room. The owner of the object must remain poker-faced so as not to give any clues about who owns it.

Step 2. If there is a low table in the center of the circle, the object can be placed there and near the selected reader. If you are the reader, this will allow you to attune yourself for a few moments before picking up the object. Let your breathing relax and allow your intuitive thinking to flow.

Step 3. When you feel ready, pick up the object and immediately start talking about its owner. Do not worry if the information is right or wrong or just plain silly. In circle you are allowed to make mistakes, for how else will you learn? It is, however, inexcusable to say nothing. Bear in mind that the first thoughts that come to your from your intuition are invariably correct. Give your impressions exactly as you receive them, without trying to censor or change the thoughts that come to you. You will have a feeling that the thoughts about the object come to you out of the blue, as if they are being given to you.

Step 4. As you hold the object let the words flow. What is the first thing you feel? Perhaps the object gives you a feeling of warmth and you may feel that the person is warm and caring. Or maybe the owner is cold and calculating? Is the person a worrier? Is he or she outgoing or tend to keep his or her own counsel? Is the owner shy, humorous, moody, witty, intelligent, talented, frustrated, bored, unfulfilled, ambitious, and so on? What does the person like doing: sports, art, walking, dancing, cooking? Ask your intuition questions, listen to your inner reply, and speak out.

Step 5. Now dig a little deeper. Some of the things you say may appear to be meaningless but may have significance to the recipient. You will get a few things wrong but the percentage you get right will increase every time you do a reading. Eventually it will come close to 100% accuracy. The important thing is to keep pushing yourself to give more and more. Believe in yourself. Trust your intuition. It is giving you correct information.

Step 6. Do not be influenced by the object itself or surmise what you think the object says about the owner. A Mickey Mouse key ring may have been bought for granny by her grandchildren, or the owner of an expensive piece of jewelry may be broke. Talk about what you feel and sense, not what you see with your eyes.

Step 7. Build a complete character profile of the owner. Say whatever comes to mind and give as much detail as you can. Speak now or you'll later regret your reluctance to speak out. Do not predict, though, as this cannot be verified immediately and, beside, psychometry is about reading vibrations from the past not the future. Have some fun with your reading: Point out the quirks and idiosyncrasies in the person's personality and see if your intuition can reveal amusing events from his or her past.

Step 8. Try to finish on a positive note, even repeating a few of the main things that felt most important. People tend to remember the first and last thing you say, so starting and finishing with strong evidence will improve your presentation. When you have finished, say so and put the object down.

When the reading is over, the group leader will ask the owner of the object to explain the percentage of what the reader got right and wrong. The recipient of the reading should go into detail, highlighting everything specific that was described. Some will be wrong but a great deal will also be startlingly accurate. If one of the group has been keeping notes, then these can be read out also. Psychometry is a comparatively easy gift to develop and you will soon discover that it is possible to progress quickly.

Psychometry helps you to develop your powers of clairsentience—the ability of clear sensing, being aware of feelings, emotions, and character traits. (I will describe this in more detail later.) Clairsentience is the glue that will hold together your mediumship. Eventually you will be able to add to this the pearls of clairvoyance (clear seeing) and clairaudience (clear hearing).

DEVELOPING THE STRUCTURE OF YOUR READING

I have explained how to do a basic psychometry reading. Once you have allowed your intuitive skills to flow, you can improve your accuracy by introducing a loose structure to the way you work.

It is important to continue to allow the information arising from your intuition to emerge unhindered and give what is received without embellishment. For example, one of my students saw a goat and went on to explain that the person was stubborn like a goat. The truth was that the person kept goats in her garden, so in this instance good evidence was lost by interference. Nonetheless, even during a stream of consciousness it is possible to monitor your messages. It is not necessary to use profanities even if the owner of the object (or a spirit communicator) used colorful language. Similarly, if you feel that something you want to say may cause offence, be upsetting, or insulting then think about what you say so as to avoid this. In addition, do not use psychometry (or mediumship) to make medical diagnoses or predictions. Talk of spirit guides and past lives is also to be avoided, as this is not verifiable and, in some instances, may be fantasy.

Your psychometry reading may be interesting to the recipient but becomes much more gripping if everyone in the room can enjoy it too. So don't mumble or leave long pauses between sentences. Try to get into a flow. This will be better for your accuracy and also make the whole session far more interesting. Interspersing a little cheerful humor will help to keep the energy from the sitters upbeat and thereby makes it easier for you to work.

An interesting psychometry reading is like a story. It has characters, motive, a plot and a beginning, middle, and end. The following headings will help you to add structure and direct your reading to make it both interesting and accurate:

Character. The easiest information to perceive with your sixth sense is the qualities of character and personality. When you first pick up an object, ask your intuition to provide you with information about the character of the current owner. If you ask, it will come. For example, is he or she an extrovert or introvert; a bubbly person or someone who looks within; shy or outspoken? Sometimes I find that while giving a reading an image of someone I already know comes to mind. The characteristics of my friend may correspond with the personality traits of the recipient of the reading. Your subconscious is telling you: "Hey, the person who owns this object is just like you friend!" So do not reject the information as your own memories—describe your friend and you will see that it corresponds with similar traits of the recipient.

Here are a few character traits that may help you with your description: honest, light-hearted, leader, expert, brave, conceited, mischievous, demanding, thoughtful, bright, outgoing, reserved, humble, friendly, adventurous, hard-working, enthusiastic, timid, shy, bold, daring, courageous, serious, funny, humorous, and sad.

Think also about what motivates the person. Are they perhaps ambitious or lazy? Can you identify their regrets and insecurities? Perhaps they hide behind a persona and put on a brave face. Are they a family person or a loner? You may also describe their physical characteristics and (with caution) any illnesses and physical weaknesses they may have had in the past.

As any writer will tell you, describing character is not as easy as it may at first seem. There is a skill to it. You need to look to the heart of the person and describe both the personality they present to the world and the person that lies within. When completely absorbed in doing a psychometry you can become so immersed that for a short while you will actually feel as if you are another person. This is when your accuracy shoots off the scale.

Life course. Begin to describe the recipient's life history. I advise my trainees to first look into the childhood of the person. Describe any pictures and scenes that come to mind. Sometimes the things you see may remind you of your own childhood, but again this is your own subconscious making comparisons and highlighting similarities. Do not reject these thoughts as unimportant, rather describe them, as they are likely to be very similar to the experiences of the recipient.

Now move forward through the recipient's life and talk about the things that have happened. Stress the emotional highlights. Can you identify any major turning points in his or her life or any secrets that nobody else knows? You may talk about the person's work life and ambitions, but events that are charged with emotions are usually most clear in our memory and will be spiritually magnetized into the energy of the object.

Talk about his or her relationships and failed relationships. Talk about the people he or she loves and hates. Again try to add detail if you can. "I see a big woman," is not enough. Ask your intuition more about her. "Oh, she was a midwife!" It is remarkable how specific the information is that comes when you remember to ask your intuition!

The present. As your reading moves through the recipient's life and to the present day, you can now add a little about current situations. Now that you are in the flow you may say a few names or include fragments of information that feel important. Do not make prophecies or give advice. You are not in training to become a counselor. You are training to eventually become a medium—someone that gives verifiable proof of the continuation of the personality after physical death.

It is easy to be distracted by people who have worldly worries, but solving these is not a medium's job. The sharing of philosophy and advice can be done after a psychometry reading but should not be done during the session. This time is to be used for giving psychic information in the case of psychometry and for receiving evidence of survival during mediumship.

Summing up. Conclude your reading by giving a brief summary of the most important things you feel about the person. Repeating the most important points about their character and life helps to reinforce what has been said and brings the reading to a natural end. Make your last sentence upbeat and positive, as this not only will be remembered but also will serve as an affirmation for the person listening.

KICK-STARTING PSYCHOMETRY

Psychometry is a sure-fire way to develop the clairvoyant skills that are the foundation of mediumship. But for many novices the hardest part is getting started. When you sit in a circle there will always be those who are too shy or self-critical to say what comes to them when they are handed an object to read. Have no sympathy for these people! I am hard on people who say, "Sorry, I am not getting anything." That is just a cop-out. We all have something in our head all of the time—the practitioner needs to say what they are thinking, feeling, or experiencing or they will not stand a chance of developing their gifts.

It is the job of the circle leader to urge hesitant readers to speak out. When someone comes up against a brick wall at the start of or during their psychometry demonstration, I push them forward by firing some questions at them. It is wise to have a few questions in mind so that you can fire them off quickly and not give the reader a chance to think about what he or she is saying. It forces the reader to give a spontaneous answer. In this way, we bypass the intellect and give the intuition a chance to work.

I may ask: "What sort of person owns the object. Is he a nice person? Do you like him?" If the answer is just "yes" then I will push further and say, "Why do you like him? What specific qualities does he have that you like?" If again the answer is numbingly obvious, such as "I don't know," I may ask: "Then how does this person remind you of yourself? Why do you relate to the object in a positive way."

As you see, I am trying to target my questions to get the practitioner to recognize qualities of the owner's character from the object. We can help by encouraging the practitioner to identify similar characteristics in him- or herself—or, as I explained earlier, by associating the impressions with the characteristics of people he or she already knows.

If the reader is still struck dumb, then have him or her answer a series of specific questions. This is veering away from the objective of describing character but for some people it helps to get them started. I may say, "Imagine you are in this person's front room. Is there a carpet on the floor and if so what color is it?" I note the response and then quickly follow with other questions, such as: "What is the owner's favorite candy? What is her favorite movie? Can she swim? Is she argumentative? Give me three Christian names that are significant to this person," and so on.

The objective is to force the reader to answer quickly and not give the person enough breathing space to think about the answers between questions. If they hesitate for even an instant, I jump on them with: "Come on, come on, quickly, quickly." It is remarkable how this simple technique can get shy people talking and working— and more often than not the results are remarkably accurate. It is also fun.

Pass the Buck

People get bored easily so it is important to make the psychometry lessons as interesting as possible. We usually kick off the start of a practice session with some simple instant psychometry. I select an object from the bag and pass it to the person next to me. The receiver is instructed to give a two- or three-sentence description of the owner or say anything that comes to mind as he or she holds the object. If the object happens to belong to that person, he or she must pretend to be reading it so that no one can guess who it really belongs to.

For this exercise there are no pauses. It is made clear to the assembled that as soon as the object touches their hand they must speak, no matter how incomprehensible or silly it may sound. Each person is to say just a few sentences and then pass it to the next person, who will also speak immediately. This is to continue until the object has quickly been passed full circle and returns to me. I make the last reading. We then ask the owner to let us know what we got right.

The speed of this exercise is important as it forces the reader to go with his or her first impressions. Sometimes I encourage others in the circle to heckle the reader to hurry up or to be more specific. One drawback, and the reason I go last, is that the timid circle members have a tendency to copy what others have said. If they do, then it is not counted as a hit and they are discouraged from mimicking one another. I praise the most adventurous readers and those with accurate information to encourage the quiet ones to be a little more daring with what they say. In this way my students gain confidence and move away from giving generalities, eventually becoming very accurate in their readings.

INTERESTING ITEMS FOR PSYCHOMETRY

You are more likely to learn a subject if you are interested in it. Right from the start it is possible to get exciting insights and achieve remarkable results from psychometry that will astonish everyone—including the person giving the message. New circles are often punctuated with: "How on earth did I get that right?" or "Wow, didn't he do well!" But it is also important to maintain this accuracy and eventually establish it as the norm. This requires lots of practice, and practice can become dull if the methods are the same every time. So to keep it interesting, I like to give my students the opportunity to approach psychometry in many different ways. This adds variety and creates interest, which increases the student's desire to learn.

As long as you know the history of an object and the character of the owner(s) you can use just about anything for psychometry. Here are a few variations on a theme that will make your psychometry evenings buzz:

Letter Psychometry

Ask visitors to the circle to bring with them letters they have received. They will need to know a little about the sender so that they can confirm or deny what is picked up about the letter. To spice it up further, add a few letters that may be charged with emotion, such as a final demand for payment, a notice of filing for divorce, a love letter, a letter from someone famous, and so on. These can be very interesting to work with during psychometry sessions.

Criminal Evidence Psychometry

A police officer or a private detective may be able to get permission for you conduct psychometry experiments on murder weapons or objects with an interesting history, such as the artifacts from museums I described earlier. Perhaps you could invite them to be your guest for the evening and ask them to bring along a few objects that have an intriguing past or an unsolved crime associated with them.

You may also want to include a few benign objects with no associated bad history—such as a brand-new carving knife straight from the shop. If you pick up no violence with this object, it would help to prove that what you are getting from the other objects is not a result of your own imagination.

Crystal Psychometry

Crystals are believed to hold vibrations and are, therefore, a very useful tool for psychometry. Before coming to the meeting each member of the circle writes down a description of an imaginary situation. This needs to include interesting imagery and be charged with emotion; for example, doing a parachute jump or driving a motorcycle through flaming hoops.

While holding a clear quartz crystal, each person now visualizes the scene. During the meditation they involve all of their five senses as well as feeling the emotions associated with what's happening in their imagined scenes. For example, if someone pictures being at sea during a raging storm, he or she may feel the rocking of the boat, shiver in the cold wind, hear the thunder, and see the gray tossing ocean. He or she would also experience the feelings of fear and excitement that would accompany such an experience. With eyes closed, the group members imagine that the images and feelings are actually happening and are being recorded by the crystal. Now they look into the crystal and imagine that they can see the scene happening inside the clear rock.

Doing this exercise imprints the quartz with the images that can be read by the psychometrists at the circle. Mark the crystals with a stick-on label and a number and put them in a bag. Each member of the circle takes a turn selecting a crystal from the bag and describing the scenes imprinted onto the crystal. I have found that holding the crystal to the third eye chakra, located at the center of the forehead, helps the reader to "see" the scenes.

My own group has had some remarkable results with this experiment. At one session I imprinted the image of a monkey sitting on top of a telegraph pole eating a banana. The reader of the crystal described this exactly!

Herb Psychometry

For this psychometry experiment, tightly seal individual fresh herbs into separate polyethylene bags and place each into a plain envelope. It is important that the fragrances of the herbs cannot be identified. For interest, include a few noxious or poisonous herbs as well. Look up the curative properties of each herb and place this information in the envelope with the appropriate herb. The reader is then asked to describe the curative or other properties of the herbs and plants hidden in the envelopes. When the reader is finished, the envelope is opened and the traditional description is read aloud to see how much the reader's analysis corresponds with the plant's traditional lore.

Flower Psychometry

Flowers are living things, and are therefore influenced by the energies of the person holding them. For this experiment each person buys a flower to bring to the circle. He or she must mark it with a stick-on label on which a symbol or design is drawn, so the individual can identify the flower as his or her own. Sometimes a raffle ticket is attached to the flower and the counterfoil kept by the owner of the flower. By carrying the flower with them to the group, each member is imprinting the aura of the flower, which can be read for psychometry. The flowers are placed in a vase in the center of the circle. As with psychometry of objects, the other people are not to know to whom each flower belongs.

When the flowers are read, the psychometrist will at first work as if reading an ordinary object: by describing the character and life of the owner. But the flower is also used as a symbol to represent the spirit of the person who brought it.

Mystics believe that nothing in the universe is coincidental. When we cast an oracle, the random cards or other divination objects are determined by the conditions of the time in which they are drawn and reflect the situation and potential future of the person who asked the question. In the same way, the flower that was chosen is also an oracle.

After the flower has been used for psychometry, the reader can interpret it as a symbol for the personality and life of owner. The stem represents the life path, with the base as the person's birth, moving upward through childhood to the top of the stem, which represents the present day.

When you read a flower it is important to observe the details. For example, if the stem is damaged at the start or has many nodules or unformed branches, then this may show a difficult start in life. A completely smooth stem may show an easy pathway through life. Watch out for bumps, breaks, and markings. All of these may indicate difficulties the flower's owner may have had.

Branches and leaves can show pathways and opportunities that have come to the person. A broken branch may represent a failed marriage or job. A bud that is damaged may represent a failed opportunity, whereas new buds may show promise for the future. The position the branch touches the stem indicates the timing for the events shown.

The way the leaves hang will show the character of the person. Leaves that hug the stem may show someone who needs security or a close-knit family. Blemishes and marks on the leaves may show problems or illnesses that a person has experienced. Look also at the overall form of the plant. Is it limp and exhausted or bright and expansive? All this says something about the owner.

The flower itself represents the person's spiritual, emotional, and intellectual aspirations. A closed flower may indicate an introverted person, whereas a splay of petals may show an extrovert. If many blooms surround a single flower it may indicate that many friends surround this person. A single flower on a leafless stem may show loneliness, or a flower with a tall stem overreaching the rest may show ambition.

The flower's colors refer to the person's emotional disposition, and the size of the bloom will give you a sense of the strength of the person's character. The center of the bloom expresses the person's innermost nature. Examine this area for flaws and interesting structures. A well-ordered center might indicate an orderly person, fine petals may show a sensitive person, and damaged stamens may mean sexual problems.

Describe your gut feelings when making your interpretation, for there are no hard and fast rules except one: Use your intuition and the correct information will come to you. The interpretation of a flower is an intuitive art. Look always beyond the structure and ask what your intuition is telling you. If you can do this you will glean remarkable information from a simple flower and give a fascinating reading.

The Envelope Game

Keeping a group active is important in order to keep everyone's interest, and the envelope game is an excellent experiment to introduce whenever the circle's energy needs a bit of a lift. My circle always enjoys this "game" because everyone is involved right from the start and there is no waiting around for someone to finish before you get your turn.

Before the meeting starts, each member of the circle is given a large envelope and a pen. They each write their name on the inside of the flap and fold it into the envelope. The envelopes are then placed on the members' laps during the meditation at the start of the session so they will absorb the vibrations of the person holding it. The members may sit on their envelopes if it is more comfortable.

After the meditation the envelopes are given to the group leader, who shuffles them and hands one to each person. The group is then asked to see what impressions they "feel" about the person who has held it earlier, and to write their own name and a couple of sentences about their personality, events from their lives and any other information about them on the top of the envelope. This is folded backward so that the next person cannot see. The envelope is then passed to the person on the left to do the same, again and so on until the envelopes have gone full circle.

The group leader now gathers the envelopes and gives them back to the original person who held them during meditation. Reading them is fascinating, as each envelope not only has impressions about that person from everyone in the group but also has a reading by that individual about the way he or she feel about him- or herself.

5 AURA MEDITATION AND SPIRIT GUIDES

"The bottom of a lake we cannot see, because its surface is covered with ripples. It is only possible for us to catch a glimpse of the bottom when the ripples have subsided and the water is calm. If the water is muddy or is agitated all the time, the bottom will not be seen. If it is clear, and there are no waves, we shall see the bottom. The bottom of the lake is our own true Self; the lake is the Chitta [mind-stuff] and the waves the Vrittis [thought-waves]."
—Swami Vivekananda

The objective of meditation is to realize your God nature. On the way to this goal you may find various treasures on the path, such as enhanced health, sharper mentality, and extrasensory powers. Meditation takes us beyond theoretical knowledge to the direct realization of the nature of existence.

Meditation teachings say we are already one with God but we are like a person who has fallen asleep to this fact. Without the realization of our God nature we experience suffering because we are trapped in the illusionary dream of separateness. We need to wake up. In our delusion we believe that the material world is the only reality and may pray to God as if "He," like the objective world, is external to ourselves. Meditation gives us a tool that can cut through this illusion. It enables us to go straight to the boss without any doctrine, priest, or guru go-betweens. Meditation awakens us to the fact that each of us is the only person who can realize our God nature. Nobody else can be enlightened for us. We are in charge of our spiritual destiny.

We will all naturally attain the goal of spiritual perfection but for most people it will take many lifetimes, as our spiritual nature evolves very gradually. Fortunately we don't have to be stuck with a long wait, for we can cultivate our spirit through meditation, unlock the yoke of ignorance, and be free to realize our God nature in this lifetime. What we do for ourselves will also help the world, for as we grow spiritually, we can assist others on the path to enlightenment, who, in turn, can help others, and so on, until one day we may actually create a utopian world.

Psychic powers are not the goal of meditation but the jewels you discover on your path to perfection. Through meditation you can develop your talents and multiply them through service to others. If psychic powers are cultivated in this spirit of service they will become very powerful and incorruptible. So when using meditation to expand your gifts, remember that they are not the final goal of your journey. They are loaned to you. You are working to become a medium, who is the conduit, not the possessor, of the power. The goal is spirituality. Mediumship is service to this spirituality.

MEDITATION AND PSYCHIC POWERS

Meditation is a natural state that you probably already have experienced without knowing it. Have you ever read a book or novel and been so totally immersed that you forgot you were reading? This is a little like meditation. It is a feeling of being absorbed, attentive, and sharply conscious. The same may have happened when listening to music. The music takes you away to "somewhere else" and for a while you are in a meditative state. It can also happen when you are in a relaxed state while doing something creative or when you are enjoying looking at a beautiful scene. It comes when you are peacefully engrossed in what you are doing.

Ideas cannot come to us when our minds swirl with hectic thoughts. Similarly, psychic and mediumistic insight cannot penetrate an agitated mind. To be aware of these things we need to achieve an inner quietude. Meditation achieves this state by calm, inner observation. It is very easy. All you need to do is sit comfortably, withdraw your attention from the day-to-day world, and give yourself a little time with your spirit. Do not be put off by the multitude of techniques available, for meditation is a natural state and can be experienced without strenuous effort. What matters is that you allow yourself to go within and observe.

Meditation is essential at the early stages of spiritual development but it is also important throughout your life as a medium. Meditation spiritualizes your work and helps to remove the hubris—the subtle spiritual arrogance that comes when mediums forget they are not the possessor but the custodians of the sacred power. It also helps you to become focused and energized and puts you in that special state of consciousness that is necessary for quality mediumship.

Meditation alone will not bring mediumship. You could meditate all of your life and the gift will still not arise if you are selfish, insensitive, egotistical, opinionated, or materialistic. However, with meditation usually comes a greater degree of self-awareness and the opportunity to improve ourselves, thereby clearing the ground for the spiritual seeds to be sown.

MEDITATION AND THE AURA

Although a medium experiences the same inner states as in traditional meditation, our objective and methodology are slightly different. We recognize that meditation is a tool for self-realization yet we also know it can be used as a way to develop mediumship.

As I have explained, the seeking of psychic powers for their own sake is a wicked, egotistic path that eventually brings ruin to those mediums who follow it. In spite of the few who mistake God's power for personal power, most mediums have integrity and are sincere in their work. So long as you embark on this journey in a spirit of modesty and compassion and maintain this throughout your work you will not stumble.

The meditation we use for the development of mediumship has many similarities to kundalini yoga but without the severe aestheticism or complicated postures. As in kundalini yoga we awaken the energy at the base of the spine and take it to the top of the head. To do this we draw upon the power of the aura and its energy centers called the chakras, which I will now describe before explaining psychic meditation in detail.

WHAT IS THE AURA?

The aura is the energy field of the life force and appears to mediums and those with clairvoyant vision as a fibrous light that surrounds living things. This ethereal light emanation also surrounds us and extends from two to three feet in all directions from the body. It is not to be confused with the lights seen by people suffering from migraine or epilepsy, cell debris in the eyes (sometimes called floaters), the bright spots of light caused when the eyes are rubbed, or the after-images caused by retinal fatigue.

Many people can sense the aura and some can see it. Have you ever stood close to a stranger and "felt" their personality—something we sometimes call the "human atmosphere"? For example, you may have visited the home of a married couple and inadvertently interrupted an argument. They may greet you with sweet smiles and pretend nothing has happened but behind this façade you can feel a pressure, like the moment before a thunderstorm. You are sensing the emotions from their auras—their projected personalities—and this is why you know that something is wrong despite their pretence. Perhaps at some time you have also experienced psychic sight and have seen the aura, but have been too embarrassed to talk about if for fear of being ridiculed by nonbelievers. Trust what you sense and see and stand by what you know to be true, for this is a natural phenomena. Fortunately many more people today are having the courage to talk about their spiritual experiences, which are proving to be more commonplace than one would have expected.

When your clairvoyant vision becomes highly developed you will notice that every human being is surrounded by auric light. The aura is brightest around the head, and this may account for why painters of Christian iconography depicted aureoles, or halos, around the heads of saints. Sometimes you may see it as a luminous cloud, like the shimmering of heat from a hot street. You will see that it is denser close to the body and becoming more tenuous and indistinct toward the peripherals. As your celestial vision sharpens you will also see the fibrous form of the aura as a dense web of fine cotton-like threads of light radiating from the body and most easily observed around the finger tips. You will note also that the aura is filled with energy and movement and that the quality of the aura changes with the mood and inner activity of the person being observed.

The Energy and Form of the Aura

The aura is a manifestation of the life force, which mediums usually refer to as *prana*—a Sanskrit term for universal energy with a literal meaning of "before breath," suggesting that it is the vital force or life essence that animates breath and gives life to the body. In the material world there are two forms of prana: the specific prana that pervades the human body and aura and the universal prana that is omnipresent, giving structure to and sustaining all things. When doing psychic meditation we not only expand and extend the aura's energy (sometimes called opening) but also draw upon this universal manifestation of the prana life force. Prana is the energy that fuels our psychic powers and is also the healing energy that is channeled by spiritual healers. (Some spirit guides, speaking through their entranced mediums, have explained that the substance of the aura is electromagnetic in nature.)

According to Eastern teachings, prana is the substance of the human aura and manifests in a number of ways and layers. The layers closest to the body are usually called the "health aura" with various layers radiating outward serving different functions. The aura is alive with energy, never static. Sometimes it can be seen as full of countless sparkling particles and may shimmer like the heat from a stove. Sometimes amidst the vibratory movement there may be seen larger balls of light, usually around the head, that indicate that the person has been involved in concentrated mental or emotional focus. The energy around the head will be seen to pulsate around people with very active brains or may be very bright around the heads of people focused on spiritual matters.

But not everyone's aura is beautiful. Some people have weak auras that draw their power from the people around them. You have probably met what we mediums call a "psychic vampire," that is, someone who unconsciously or consciously draws from the energy of stronger persons. These people sap your life energy and leave you feeling drained. The auras of ill people will be less vibrant and clouded; in an angry person's aura you may even see what looks like flames; and in depressed people the normally bright, straight fibrous quality of the auric light becomes dull and wilts like a plant starved of nourishment.

Colors of the Aura

The prana that comprises the aura is colorless—like clear water or glass—but becomes colored by our thoughts and emotions. Mediums with a well-developed spiritual vision will be aware of these colors and how they change. As these colors require clairvoyance to be seen, they are know as astral colors.

The aura is painted from a palette of astral colors made from the three primary colors: red, blue, and yellow. From a mixture of these all the other colors are formed. The primary color red represents the physical world, blue the spiritual, and yellow the mental; while white stands for purity and black for negativity. (Black is not a color but is the absence of light and white is the harmonious blending of the astral colors.)

As a general rule the bright colors seen in an aura have a positive diagnosis, as they indicate a happy disposition. The duller tones show moodiness, illness, and depression.

The following list explains some of the colors you will see in the aura, but remember when working with and interpreting the aura that your own intuition will tell you most about the person. The colors of the aura are affected by thoughts and emotions—try to look beyond the colors to the thoughts and feelings that also bathe in the aura's light. The colors you see may trigger a gut feeling in you that is likely to correspond with the thoughts and emotions of the person you are observing.

Red (primary color)
Red is the color of physical energy and the activities associated with the vitality of the body, such as athletic or sexual activity. A clear, clean shade of red indicates friendship, vitality, determination, and vigor, but if it is tainted with darker shades this shows selfishness and coarse passion. Anger may cause a red light to flash through the aura, whereas sensitivity and kindness manifests as a gentle pink tone. The aura of a pregnant woman is usually pink but that does not necessarily mean the baby will be a girl.

Orange
The color orange combines the power of red with the intellect of yellow and can indicate intellectual ambition, mastery of will, and pride. It may show a desire for change and breaking from the past. Balls of orange light in the aura indicate that the person has been concentrating on a number of issues. Orange is also linked to the spleen area and shows healing though spiritual cleansing.

Yellow (primary color)
Yellow is an energetic color associated with intellectual activities and creative self-expression. If these aspirations are inspired then the aura around the head will become a nimbus of golden yellow, sometimes edged with a blue tint. If seen as many fine moving lines, it shows the subject's mental activities are many and varied. This fibrous effect may reveal a worrier even though yellow generally is an optimistic color.

Green
Often found in the auras of spiritual healers, green lies in the center of the astral spectrum and indicates balance. It is nature's color and is associated with renewal and recovery. Green combines the intellectual creativity of yellow with the spirituality of blue. Bright spring green will indicate someone who actively likes to help others, whereas a sickly lemon-green reveals deceit and envy. Rich emerald tones show reliability, strength of character, and a well-balanced personality.

Blue (primary color)
Blues are the spiritual colors of the astral palette. Blue stands for high ideals, altruism, devotion, reverence, and religious aspirations. It is

considered to be the healing color, as blue calms and brings peace. Blue is associated with the sky and feelings of freedom and escape from restriction. An aura dominated by blue indicates that the person is healthy and at peace.

Indigo and Violet

Indigo and violet are a continuation of the spiritual aspects of the color blue. Although sometimes associated with depression, indigo is also a sign of clairvoyant ability and an intuitive person who may be inspired by their dreams. Purple will show love of ceremony and deep religious conviction. Violet is the highest of the spiritual blues, showing a person who has integrated their higher nature.

Black, White, Silver, and Gold

Black is not a color but the absence of light. Nonetheless, sometimes the aura does show dark clouds. These usually indicate depression, negativity, and lack of energy. A heavy overshadowing of black stands for hatred, malice, and a vengeful disposition. White indicates the opposite and is a sign of purity of heart, good character, and a positive attitude. When white is seen as rays within any of the auric colors it adds opulence to the aura and shows a high degree of spiritual attainment. Silver expresses spiritual sincerity as well as quick thinking, mental agility, and, to a lesser extent, humor. Gold is considered by some to be the color of protection.

THE AURA AND CHAKRAS IN PSYCHIC MEDITATION

When we meditate for mediumistic development our physical and spiritual bodies go through a number of important changes that enable us to become sensitive to the spirit world. At first these changes may be a little uncomfortable, and sometimes you may be a little oversensitive. You may respond to the anxieties and fears of other people and pick up their stress and general mental condition. As you progress it will get easier and you will discover how to regulate your sensitivity. This is one of the primary reasons we work with the aura during meditation, for the aura is a spiritual doorway that we can open or close at will.

The aura has a number of focuses of spinning energy called *charkas*, a Sanskrit word meaning wheel. The seven main charkas correspond to the endocrine glands of the body and run upward along the spinal chord. They connect the physical body to the etheric body, which is said to be the psychophysical bridge between the earthly and ethereal worlds. Some see the chakras as swirling vortexes of light, while others describe them as lotuses with varying numbers of petals or like a spiral galaxy of stars.

Chakras are focal points for the flow of prana energy through the body and help to maintain our health. Each chakra is associated with different functions of the body and is linked to the channels called *nadis* (a Sanskrit word meaning movement) that carry the prana energy through the physical body and, particularly for our purposes, from the base of the spine to the crown of the head. Each chakra on the front of the body is paired with its counterpart on the spine; together they are considered the front and rear aspects of one chakra.

The seven charkas also have qualities that come into play when a specific chakra center is vitalized through meditation. The lower chakra centers are linked with the body and the higher centers with spiritual qualities. As the energy rises up the spine and through the different charkas it transmutes into spiritual energy, eventually reaching its perfection at the crown chakra at the top of the head. When we raise the energy from the base of the spine to the top of the head we trigger the spiritual energies required to enter states of higher consciousness. Simultaneously the aura expands and enables our inner world to resonate with the higher vibrations of the spirit world. For our immediate purpose, what is most important is the meditation that begins the journey of the prana light from the base center to the top of the head.

As with meditation, spirituality cannot be attained simply by applying a method. The chakras activate when the practitioner realigns his thinking, stops hurting people, stops being selfish, and so on. Working with the chakras will prepare your body for the coming of spiritual powers so long as the appropriate work has also been done on the self.

The Meaning of the Chakras

Base/Root Center (red light)
Sanskrit name: Muladhara (root/support)
This is the seat of the spiritual energy located at the base of the spine and is the source of our physical strength and vitality. It is the powerhouse that provides the cosmic energy to drive the other charkas. It is associated with the survival drive and instincts and has the element earth. (Practicality) The root chakra identifies with the adrenal glands.

Sacral Center (orange light)
Sanskrit name: Svadhisthana (sweetness)

This center is situated below the navel and refines and filters the cosmic energy. It is associated with emotions and has the element water. (The emotions) Water: The sacral chakra identifies with the gonads.

Solar Plexus Center (yellow light)
Sanskrit name: Manipura (lustrous jewel)
Situated below the rib cage, the solar plexus is the storehouse of psychic energy. It is associated with the ego and has the element fire. (Energy) The solar plexus chakra identifies with the pancreas.

Heart Center (green light)
Sanskrit name: Anahata (unstruck)
The heart center is located in the center of the chest and close to the heart. This is the highest of the emotional centers and is associated with relationships. It has control of the chakra centers below and converts instinct into feeling. The heart chakra identifies with the thymus gland. Its element is air. (Mind)

Throat Center (blue light)
Sanskrit name: Visshudha (purification)
Located at the top of the throat, this is the first of the three main spiritual centers. This center is associated with creative and is used by mediums during clairaudience (spiritual hearing). The throat chakra identifies with the thyroid gland. Its element is ether. (Spirit)

Forehead/Brow Center (indigo light)
Sanskrit name: Ajan (to perceive)
Also known as the "third eye," this chakra is located in the center of the forehead. Through this center clairvoyance is received. The forehead center works in tandem with the throat and crown chakras to provide psychic insights. The forehead center identifies with the pituitary gland. Its element is sound. (Soul)

Crown Center (violet light)
Sanskrit name: Sahasrara (thousandfold)
In the East this center at the top of the head is know as the "thousand-pedaled lotus" and although associated with the color violet is in reality a kaleidoscope of colors. Thoughts and projected thought forms radiate from this center, taking on astral colors. For example, an angry thought will be colored red, a creative thought yellow, a spiritual thought blue, and so on. Thoughts also have form, which can be seen by people with advanced celestial vision as intricate geometrical patterns. The crown chakra of a spiritually advanced person will be seen to form into an astonishing

mandala of lights with patterns, shapes, and colors reminiscent of a peacock's fanned tail. The crown center is the center of our awareness and connects us to the divine. It is identified with the pineal gland and has the element of Light. (God)

PREPARING FOR MEDITATION

Circle of Protection

Soon we are going to raise the prana light from the chakra at the base of the spine to the crown chakra at the top of the head so that we can enter psychic meditation. Raising the energy in this way increases our sensitivity to spirit and expands the aura. As this happens the aura also opens—that is, it becomes sensitized to subtle vibrations (including the objects you may use in psychometry), to other people, and also to the spirit communicators. At this time other people's thoughts and feelings of jealousy, anger, hatred, and so on can deeply affect us. We are also subject to depletion of energy if we are in contact with people who are ill, so it is important that we choose the time and setting for this meditation carefully.

During everyday life we are unaware of the vibrations surrounding us. If our auras were expanded and open all the time, negative vibrations would soon deplete us. Intense people or those with severe mental problems project thought forms that would influence our auras and could affect us deeply and undermine our inner harmony. Our auric energy may also be sapped by the "psychic vampires" I mentioned earlier. This is why a medium, on finishing work, allows his or her aura to quiet down and "close." Furthermore, an expanded aura requires high energy levels that cannot be sustained by the novice. Only the advanced spiritual adept, such as a yogi who has renounced worldly activity, would be safe remaining in this state all the time.

When I am not working as a medium I allow my aura—and with it my psychic awareness—to rest in what many mediums call a closed state. The terms "opening the aura" and "closing the aura" are commonly used and frequently misunderstood. In reality the aura cannot close completely. If it did we'd be dead, for we'd have no life force. The aura is not a solid object that opens wide or slams shut to close. When we talk of opening, it is an energizing and expanding of the aura. Closing is a quieting of the aura, as in normal day-to-day awareness. During these times of inactivity the energy is recharging so that when the time comes to meditate or practice mediumship I can draw on considerable amounts of renewed prana energy.

Soon I will explain how to open the aura and also how to close it again after your session.

If you are a sincere medium and working with the prana light for the benefit of others, your psychic powers will be active and you will be receptive to vibrations, but you cannot be harmed by other people's negative energy or by intruding entities. Even when you enter haunted houses or places with a negative vibration you are completely protected, for darkness cannot penetrate light.

If there are times when you feel the need to protect your aura, you can arm yourself using the auric light. A wash of red drawn into the aura can increase vitality and protect your from illness. Red is a color that naturally occurs in sports people and doctors. Orange and yellow auric light will protect the intellect and may be drawn upon during arguments or debates. The blue group of colors, including purples and violets, will protect the spirit. Blues and purples are the colors found in the auras of spiritual people, moral teachers, and people with lofty ideals. All these colors are of the spirit and soul and will protect you from low vibrations and influences. When the aura is infused with the appropriate color it will rebound negative emotions, thoughts, and energies.

Mediums also speak of the higher levels of protection—sometimes called the "great auric circle." As we develop our spiritual gifts, we spontaneously build a powerful aura in the astral world that acts as an infallible shield to all forms of psychic attack on all planes of existence. This has been described as a circle but is, in effect, egg-shaped or oval, for it surrounds the aura as a shell encases an egg. It is made of pure white pranic light and has the power of all the worldly aura colors combined. The white light is the radiation of the spirit, which is higher than the ordinary mind, emotion, or body and before which all negative vibrations disintegrate. It is the armor of the soul.

Moving the Light in Meditation

I have stressed that the goal of meditation is divine consciousness. This will always be the foundation of your work, but the specific remit of a medium requires special techniques that while rooted in traditional meditation have a slightly different focus. You will enter the deep contemplative states to discover the meaning of your life and your true nature but you will also use some of your meditative time to commune with the spirit guides and helpers. This is not unique to spiritualist mediums. In India they say that if the guru cannot be found in this life then he may connect to the seeker through the astral planes.

I will now help you to establish this rapport with the spirit teachers and show you how to safely enter the meditative states that are conducive for mediumship. You may want to glance at chapter two again to refresh your memory about the basics of sitting for meditation and how the group can be structured. I have also already described the sequence for a group meditation as well as the importance of seating, posture, and breathing.

Step 1: The group leader may begin by ringing a bell and saying some soothing words to lead you into meditation. Sit comfortably and with your eyes closed, notice how your breathing is slowing down. Enjoy watching the breath for a while as your mind enters a peaceful state of contemplation.

Step 2: See below you an ocean of brilliant white light. This is the infinite prana energy that can be tapped during meditation. You are floating above this ocean of light. Now draw this energy toward the first chakra, which lies at the base of the spine. As the light comes to this base center feel it swirling with energy. The chakra opens like a flower of light. You may see red light here, which is the designated color for this chakra.

Step 3: Now draw the light up to each chakra one at a time, finishing with the crown chakra at the top of the head that opens in a mandala of light—like a brilliant jeweled fan of peacock's feathers. Return each time to the sea of light below and draw energy. As the light enters each chakra see them open like flowers of light and vibrate with brilliant lights in the colors associated with each chakra. The charkas are now vitalized by the prana energy being drawn upward from the base of the spine to the top of the head. Some people experience this as a moving double helix of light running upward and spiraling through the charkas and up the spine to the top of the head.

Step 4: Now that the charkas are open, visualize a glorious sun of light above you. Its golden rays shine though you and shower you with light. As the light floods through your body it washes away all negativity. This process purifies the aura and prepares the astral body for communication with the spirit.

Step 5: Once you feel the light has done its job, allow the light from above to fill your whole body with light. You may imagine it as liquid light pouring in through the crown chakra and filling the body like a vessel from the soles of the feet to the top of the head, which is now open like a glorious mandala of light.

Step 6: As the cosmic light fills your body you will feel the energy moving into your aura, which now expands and links with the others meditating with you and to the spirit people from the next life who are helping you. The merging of the lights flowing up through the base chakra and down from the crown chakra create a powerful spiritual force. At this point you may become aware of how your auric light is at one with the omnipresent divine light. You may merge with the light and experience the wonderful inner peace and joy that accompanies this realization.

If done properly, the aura meditation I have just described will naturally induce a state of inner peace. You will feel energized and relaxed. You are now ready to begin meditation.

Once the practice of opening the aura has become habitual, a medium may instantaneously open by giving the inner command: "I am now opening my chakras and aura." A similar inner command may be used to close the aura. Novices may want to experiment with imagery, such as visualizing a bag being unzipped, opening a door, or an expanding light. A photographer who sat in my circle used to imagine a lens aperture opening over each chakra.

PSYCHIC MEDITATION

Modern psychology recognizes that people think in different ways and that their thinking is related to one or more of the five senses. Similarly, there are many meditation methods available that will suit different personality types, so do not be concerned if your own inner experience does not exactly match what I am about to describe. Go with the flow and allow yourself to become naturally immersed in the meditation in the way that suits you best. The meditation will help you to let go of tension, anxiety, and depression and you will move toward feelings of peace, optimism, and self-worth. Energy, stability, and tranquility will be carried forward into your life. So enjoy the experience rather than worry unduly about technique.

At first you may fidget and find that your mind won't relax, but over the weeks there will be a gradual disciplining of the body and mind and you will be able to sit for longer periods. You will be alert, focused, concentrated, and very relaxed, but do not allow yourself to fall asleep. Although no harm will come to you it will, however, be to the detriment of the others, as this will disrupt the flow of energy in the circle—besides, your snoring will be distracting. (I have been tempted to keep a water pistol by my side for such occasions!)

During meditation you will remain attentive but not immersed in the clatter of daily thinking and the endless loop of internal dialogue. When people first sit for meditation they think that their thoughts are speeding up, but what is really happening is that they are becoming aware of how hectic their normal thinking is. Most people have no control over their thinking and even less over their emotions. During meditation we gain inner peace and self-control by stepping back from our daily thoughts. Instead of being drawn by every whim rattling around our head, our consciousness becomes relaxed yet powerfully focused. To achieve this extraordinary inner state, all we need to do is watch the thoughts.

The aura technique has prepared the ground for your meditation. Now by separating yourself from your thinking you transcend the everyday mind and attune yourself with what Western mystics call the "overself"—the higher you that extends into the afterlife and beyond. It is centered in the eternal now. Witnessing the flow of the mind can bring you to a transcendent state of awareness which allows the deeper aspects of meditation to unfold revealing the true nature of the self as pure consciousness.

Step 1: Watch your thoughts like film images flashing on the screen of your attention. Observe them but do not follow them. If you find that you have slipped back into a stream of thought, bring your attention back and continue to observe. You do not need to suppress thoughts or the feelings that come to you. Simply observe them and let them go.

Step 2: If emotions well up, note them and let them go. Remind yourself of the fact that these issues can be dealt with later but that for now you are focused on more important things.

Step 3: Sometimes your thoughts will express themselves as visions. Just as in dreams some may be pleasant and others ugly. Detach from these too—observe them and let them go. Even if these visions contain interesting prophecies or clairvoyance, let them go. Focus on being the unattached watcher.

Step 4: If there are sounds in the vicinity, such as a ticking clock in the hall, let these distractions be part of your observation. Observe them and let them go.

Step 5: Eventually you will be free from distractions and will enter a peaceful yet alert state of consciousness. Meditation is like sleep, it cannot be taught. It is something that comes by itself and only afterward do you realize you have been meditating.

With practice meditation will become an established habit and you will quickly be able to enter it every time you sit in circle. It is a state you can carry forward into everyday life and brings with it the benefits of inner peace, emotional stability, and intellectual sharpness. I am reminded of the words of the controversial guru Sai Baba, who asks his devotees to use their wristwatch as a spiritual trigger: "When you watch the watch, remember the five letters of the word *watch*," says Sai Baba. "Each is giving you a fine lesson of life: **W** tells you to 'watch your words'; **A** warns you to 'watch your actions'; **T** indicates to 'watch your thoughts'; **C** advises, 'watch your character'; and **H** declares 'watch your heart.' When you are consulting your watch, imbibe this lesson that the watch is imparting."

The peaceful inner states that you enter during meditation are beneficial to your body, mind and spirit. Time spent in meditation is for you so do not worry unduly that you are not always in communication with your spirit guides or experiencing meaningful visions. Meditation is a simple process with many powerful benefits. It is your time for your own personal development and to recharge your spirit.

Most of the time, particularly when you work alone, you will use meditation for personal spiritual growth. However, there are also a number of purposeful inner techniques that can be incorporated into your group meditation. Eastern traditions employ specific meditation techniques to evoke special powers such a bilocation, astral projection, lucid dreaming, awareness of subliminal sound, control of the autonomic nervous system, and many other miraculous abilities. The technique you have learned to open the chakras and aura increases your sensitivity and enables you to become attuned to the influences of your spirit guides and loved ones who have passed over. At the appropriate time, that is, when you are ready, the spirit may draw close to you and give you guidance. But do not anticipate a blinding-light-on-the-road-to-Damascus type of experience. The spirit will come gently, like a quiet, almost imperceptible, voice that whispers words of hope across the great silence of your meditation.

At my own circle I now divide the meditation into two sections—a method you may wish to try sometimes. The first part the meditation is dedicated entirely to oneself. We go into the meditative state and simply enjoy the experience. I then ask my students to return to normal awareness and quickly ask them to return to meditation but now "sit for spirit." During this second stage of our attunement we open our minds to the spirit world and communicate with our guides. Messages may be given to us for others sitting in the room, and which can be discussed later. If we have a guest present we ask of spirit that the information we are given is specifically for them.

While sitting for spirit, occasionally the students are permitted to make short notes in their spiritual diaries. For example, they may "hear" the name of a spirit communicator or receive information or imagery. A short note or keyword is put in the notebook to help recall. It is fascinating if more than one person writes down the same information, such as a name or an image that is then confirmed to be significant by the guest. These instances indicate that telepathy and/or spirit communication is taking place.

SITTING FOR SPIRIT

When the mind is still it becomes like a pool that ripples when even the smallest petal lands on its surface. This inner stillness gives the spirit people the opportunity to communicate with you directly. They send you a thought and you will be aware of it rippling across the surface of your consciousness. Just as you are aware of your own thoughts and can observe them, you are now aware of thoughts coming from outside of yourself.

The spirit guides and helpers will not take you over against your will nor force themselves upon you. Only once you have given your consent will they will begin the inner communication, and they will progress gently and only at your pace. They do not jump into you or have you spitting green slime at the ceiling. If at any stage you feel uncomfortable, just ask them to step back and they will do so immediately.

Working with the spirit is a partnership. At no time is a medium overshadowed to the point that he or she is out of control or looses his or her sense of what is right or wrong. You may be in a highly receptive state but you are always the one in the driver's seat.

The spirits communicate in many ways, and the experience may differ from person to person. Sometimes I have the feeling that a thought has been given to me like an idea that has come from out of the blue. Sometimes I may see pictures that describe an idea in a symbolic way; occasionally I sense inner sounds, but most of the time my meditations are accompanied by a blissful feeling of being enveloped in the love and compassion of the spirit. We are truly blessed to be honored by the advanced souls who have come to help us.

For me the clarity of inner spiritual rapport comes when I realize that I am having an inner dialogue with the spirit communicators. This happens spontaneously and, in my own case, I have noticed that it often follows a period of sleepiness that sometimes follows the alertness of the initial meditation. It is an inner dialogue not with myself but with a real spirit person who can tell me things that can be verified later. Because I have worked as a medium for many years, it is clear to me which are my own thoughts and which have been given to me by the spirit. The novice medium will find it hard initially to make this distinction, and will sometimes confuse their own thoughts with those from outside themselves. With experience you will learn to identify which are your own thoughts and which are those coming to you from another source.

With practice you will learn to observe not only your own thoughts but also thoughts that are not your own. The stillness of meditation is the place to begin this work. Through inner observation you will learn to recognize the spirit thoughts and, eventually, be able to engage in a dialogue with the spirit friends. At first this will be during meditation, but as your skill increases you will come to recognize spirit thoughts during normal awareness, particularly when you are demonstrating your skills as a medium.

Conversations with Spirit Guides

Spirit guides have proven their existence many times through trance mediumship and been photographed when they have materialized at physical séances. You may become aware of the influence of your guides when they draw close during meditation and you may feel tremendously inspired by the beauty and radiance of their personality. They are real beings—advanced souls who have postponed their merger into infinite bliss in order to return to us to teach us spiritual knowledge.

Spiritualists prefer to call them guides rather than angels because their function is to work with a specific individual or small group of individuals. People who make outlandish claims about the status of their guide are usually lost in an ego-based fantasy. I am reminded of Britain's most famous spiritualist guide, named Silver Birch, who was the American Indian control of the medium Maurice Barbanell, the editor of *Psychic News* and a famous journalist in his time (1902–81).

The inspiring words, wisdom, and evidence given by Silver Birch have, in my opinion, never been surpassed and was acclaimed by the great Spiritualist pioneers Lord Dowding, Sir Arthur Conan Doyle, Arthur

Findlay, and Sir Oliver Lodge, and yet neither Barbanell nor Silver Birch ever made any claim to him being the "highest of the high."

Silver Birch told of a hierarchy of spirits working together to enable communication and that he had to "lower" his vibration in order to communicate with the material world. In turn, "the masters" have to lower their vibrations in order to communicate with him. Silver Birch explained that the Indian guide the masters talk to is an "astral shell" through which he communicates to us. In reality, he is not an Indian at all but a being of light speaking to us through the spiritual persona we call Silver Birch.

When a medium claims to be in touch with the archangels or have a guide that is so many hundreds of thousands of years old, for me at least, alarm bells go off. If, in addition, the medium's channeling fails to inspire, is impossible to verify, or verges on psychobabble, then I head for the exit. It is not the guide that is important but the words, wisdom, and verifiable information that come through the guide that counts. Therefore, do not be distracted by the form the guide shows you. A tangible form is maintained so that we can distinguish between the many beings of light that communicate with us.

Working with Your Guide

Much of your inner work will be done with spirits you already know. The spirit of a dead parent or grandparent may be one of your first helpers. Once an internal dialogue is established with these spirits, you will gradually notice that others now draw close to help.

The first guide you are likely to become aware of is called the "gatekeeper," whose guiding hand has been with you from birth. He or she will also be the guide who will escort you into the next life when it is time to die. The gatekeeper will instruct you and give you insight into your spiritual direction and will help you to awaken your spiritual powers. In addition, guides who have specific tasks to perform will also draw close. Guides may appear who will help you when working with children or young people; others will help you channel healing, use ESP, or be the conduit for physical mediumship, transfiguration, and trance mediumship.

The guides will come as they are needed and many of these will have a special purpose. For example, if the arts are used in your psychic work you will attract guides to help with psychic portraiture, inspired music, or writing. Often when I am demonstrating to an audience I sense a clown guide working with me, who will seek out amusing stories I can include in my evidence of survival. His role is important, as a sprinkling of humor helps to raise the vibration and energy levels of the audience, which, in turn, fuels my mediumship.

When sitting for spirit you will sense that your guide is with you. He or she will not try to take you over or force any information on you. You will not, for example, be shown how or when you will die or be given distressing information. The guide will work with you at your pace and will neither push you too hard nor give in to demands that you may make. He or she helps to water the inner garden, and when the time is right the flowers will bloom.

Allowing your guides to sprinkle their thoughts across the screen of your awareness prepares you for full mediumship. If one day you are praised you for your spiritual work, you will know it is the spirit guides that do the real work. It is they who establish the inner rapport with, and bring to you and organize, the thousands of spirits who will, during the course of your mediumship, send messages of hope to countless people through you.

Becoming Aware

When a guide's thoughts are superimposed on your own it is know as a light "overshadowing," or "influence." You will notice that you are fully conscious and in control and have the option to return to normal consciousness whenever you want to. All mediumship is based upon this blending of thought. Even when you are doing a private reading and chatting to the sitter there is a slight overshadowing as the spirit people pass to you the information for the client.

During meditation or when sitting for spirit you may have a glimpse of someone who was known to you and who loved you, such as a spouse or a parent. These clairvoyant visions may make you feel happy and inspired. Your thoughts are potent forces that will be received by those in the spirit, even if you are not aware that they have "heard" you. Do not bombard your guides with a stream of requests. You may, of course, ask the occasional question, but the answer may not always come immediately. You will get a reply when you are ready to receive it, perhaps during another meditation session or sometime during the next day when you are in a contemplative mood.

Your most important insights will come in the form of a silent influence, as the guides blend with your awareness. They will help you to develop your clairvoyance and also help you to overcome your negative traits, inspire you in times of crisis, help you rid yourself of selfishness, and enable you to become a better person.

TARGETED INNER EXPERIMENTS

During most meditation session you will enter the peaceful states I have described earlier and sometimes attune yourself to the thoughts of the spirit people. There will be times when you will feel no spirit influences around you at all but will, nonetheless, enjoy the benefits of meditation for its own sake. During circle you will be given what you need at the time. You will also notice that the energy in the room will change from week to week. Sometimes everyone will feel tired at the onset of meditation, so the spirit helpers will spend their time lifting the energy and revitalizing you. There will be times also when you collectively are given information, such as a shared vision or a communication from a specific circle guide.

What follows is a series of meditation experiments that can be used occasionally after the main meditation and as an alternative to the sitting for spirit section. The experiments help to verify your inner experiences as coming from spirit by revealing corresponding content to other members of your group.

Eidetic Visualization

Traditional meditation holds the mind steady, but for mediumistic meditation we sometimes need to encourage and work with a stream of creative thought. For this experiment we will relax, watch the breath, and step back from the thoughts and observe them. Without allowing ourselves to fall into sleep, we will stimulate a state of drowsiness similar to what psychologists call hypnagogic dreaming.

Hypnagogic dreams are extremely vivid images that some people experience as they are dropping off to sleep and sometime—though much more rarely—as they are waking up (hypnopompic dreaming). These are forms of lucid dreaming in which you remain awake as the dream is taking place. The dreams are incredibly real and include an astonishing flow of strange patterns, scenes, and imagery. These extraordinary visual images are referred to as being eidetic. When I experience this state I am awed by the effortless way the unconscious conceives of such complex, labyrinthine images that would take the Disney Studios centuries to animate. Yet these visions appear out of nowhere.

This waking dream state can be triggered during meditation and is a useful source of clairvoyant material. Hypnagogic dreaming is a state of intermediate consciousness preceding sleep that can be triggered and sustained during meditation without falling into sleep. This is not a method you need practice every time you mediate but it is a useful step that helps you to become attuned to your unconscious and its intuitive powers.

Sometimes the hypnagogic state occurs spontaneously during meditation. It may come and go so quickly that you only glimpse it. At other times you may recognize the state and be able to sustain it for an extended period. I have noticed that some of my circle sitters will consistently be whisked of f on all sorts of fantastic adventures when they meditate. Although these visionary journeys provide interesting insights, they can become a distraction from the goal of our work, which is a clear communication with the spirit that is unfettered by symbolism.

Step 1: A session of eidetic meditation begins with the circle leader explaining the material I just touched on and suggesting that during meditation everyone focus on visual imagery.

Step 2: When you meditate you will probably see a spontaneous image appear in the mind's eye. Look at it closely and let it hold your attention. Make the image more vivid by observing everything you can about it. Get all of the senses involved, particularly visual perception. Perhaps you can shift your attention to a different vantage point, such as above or below the image, or you may be able to zoom in to or out from the vision.

Step 3: If you see a face, look more closely at the details: the fall of the hair, the color of the eyes, the pores of the skin, and so on. Similarly, if you see a landscape, move toward it and see every tiny detail.

Step 4: Gently concentrate on an image as it arises and hold it for a few moments in the screen of your attention until it becomes vivid. Then let it go and allow another spontaneously generated picture to come. It is likely to appear almost immediately. Again look hard at it and examine it carefully in your mind's eye.

Step 5: Now let that picture go and allow another to come, and another, until you can clearly see a stream of ever-changing images flowing through your awareness. If the images do not come just relax and try again. Keep the attention focused yet simultaneously allow your stream of consciousness to flow effortlessly.

Step 6: Remembering what you have seen is quite difficult, for just like a dream the images will fade as soon as you enter normal awareness, so when you come out of meditation immediately write down what you can recall from your visions.

This type of meditation gets really interesting when you compare notes afterward. You will find that many in your circle have had the same visions—sometimes down to the tiniest details. These pictures may be unconscious material that has been shared between you using telepathy but often also will include material given to you by the spirit guides. Sometimes a number of you will see the same spirit guides come to you and show or tell you similar things. This is one way the guides verify their reality, not just within the group but sometimes between different circles working in different locations.

The imagery seen during meditation can be interpreted as symbols just as you would interpret the symbolism from a dream. However, the symbols, allegories, and metaphors entwined in the images are of a higher order than dreams, for they usually deal not with your anxieties and emotional problems but with the highest aspirations of your soul. Interpreting the imagery may help you to reveal your spiritual path and give you insight into the higher purpose of your life.

Other things you can try during meditation and compare notes on may include:

Moving the Energy

When you sit in meditation you will become aware of how the energy in the room shifts. You may feel it move in a clockwise or counterclockwise direction. Sometimes it may appear high or low or may feel centered around a particular member of the group. Compare notes afterward and you will see correlations between what you all have been feeling. Noticing similar shifts in the energy will verify that your experience is not imagination but the movement of real energy.

Meeting One Another

Before the experiment begins the group leader teams the circle members into pairs. During the meditation you and your partner will try to meet one another during your visualization. For example, if you see a landscape look for your circle friend. Perhaps the guides will tell you or show you something. Afterward compare notes: You will be amazed at how many of the images and events that occured during your meditation are the same. You both even may have received a similar message from a spirit guide or dead relative. If a dead relative is confirmed when the meditation is being discussed afterward, then this is an opportune moment to practice a mediumistic link and see if the person receiving the vision can add more detail by way of a reading.

A variation on this method is for everyone in the circle to focus on just one sitter during the meditation and give him or her a message afterward. This may be particularly appropriate if you have a guest for the session. Sometimes the best mediumship comes during the meditation session, and it is much less intimidating for the novice to describe information received during meditation than to work face to face with a person. A little correct information received during meditation that is verified afterward can give a great boost to the confidence and act as a catalyst that leads to a full and accurate reading.

Some of the techniques I have suggested tap the powers of the unconscious mind and can be of benefit so long as we remain realistic. I discourage fantasy and anything that could lead to group hallucination. In my work I have crossed swords via the *Daily Express* newspaper and the *Psychic News* with the TV illusionist Derren Brown. On TV he cleverly demonstrated that a carefully selected and susceptible group of people sitting in a "séance" could be tricked into believing that they have seen real Spiritualist phenomena. Brown used a number a psychological techniques including suggestion, conjuring, and direct hypnotism to influence the proceedings. I argued that just because a carefully selected group fall for his mind games, doesn't mean that all Spiritualist séances are chicanery. It is important that clarity and a sensible even-minded approach is maintained at all times.

TIME TO CLOSE DOWN

When you have finished working you will need to quiet the aura and chakras. If you were to remain open and psychically sensitive all of the time, your energy would quickly become depleted. You would also be defenseless to every negative vibration or thought that comes your way. Once this next technique becomes an established habit, closing will be much quicker and you will automatically return to normalcy when you are finished. However, the novice needs to practice this technique, and it needs to be the standard way to close your circles. Visitors and guests at your circle, whether or not they are clairvoyant, will also need to close down, as their auras, too, will naturally expand during the session. Closing down is the safe way to conclude a circle.

Step 1: Sit comfortably and allow the breath to quiet. Feel a gentle peace pervade your body and aura.

Step 2: Focus your attention on the brow chakra and feel the light fade. The petals of the lotus close and the center becomes still.

Step 3: Now do the same for throat, heart, solar plexus, and spleen chakras. The light fades, the centers become still, and as the lotus flowers close the centers return to normality.

Step 4: The base chakra does not close completely. See the light here fade until it is just a small red light—like a chink of light through a partly opened door.

Step 5: The crown chakra at the top of the head is still open. As you did when you opened, see a golden sun above you and allow the light to shower through you, except this time keep all the other chakras closed. Give yourself a cosmic shower of light and when you feel fully cleansed fill the body with light from the toes to the top of the head.

Step 6: Now close the crown chakra. The fan of light folds and the energy retracts and becomes still.

Step 7: Quickly run through the chakra centers again to make sure they are all quiet. Now, as a final safeguard, visualize wrapping a warm, dark blanket around your body and over your head. Use this image to pull the aura back to the body as you return to normal consciousness. You are now fully awake and refreshed.

Step 8: If you are driving home, allow a little time afterward for the aura to normalize. Have a refreshing drink and a chat about the intriguing evening you have just enjoyed.

6 MEDIUMISTIC DEVELOPMENT

"The greatest problem in the world today is intolerance. Everyone is so intolerant of each other."
—Princess Diana

You don't plan to become a medium—it's something that happens. In my own instance I certainly didn't choose this path, and of the many mediums I know I am sure most would agree that it was not something they sought either. I believe there is a cosmic plan working in the background of the lives of mediums. It draws us with an irresistible magnetism back to the spiritual path and sometimes does this whether we like it or not!

When my mediumship first developed I used to keep it a secret from my friends and particularly from the customers at my graphic advertising business .As a single parent I also had to watch my step, as it easily could be misconstrued that I was delving into something sinister. I rarely worked locally and used to travel some distance to demonstrate my gift at London-based Spiritualist churches. These were far from my hometown and so ensured that people I knew would not see me. In those not-so-distant days people still thought Spiritualists to be odd people who sat in darkened séance rooms to call up the dead. In fact, in the U.K. the practice of mediumship was illegal until 1951 and mediums were put in jail if caught demonstrating.

In recent years there has been a massive change of attitude. Some journalists and skeptics call us scoundrels and denounce us all as charlatans, but the general public is becoming a little more thoughtful about these issues and many now recognize that most mediums are sincere, gifted people. The cause has been helped by a number of public figures and celebrities who have spoken out on our behalf and helped bring greater acceptance of mediumship in society at large. Perhaps no one did more to focus the world's attention on Spiritualism than Princess Diana, who, during her short life, visited a great many mediums, healers, and psychics. An employee who was also a close confidant of the princess told me that she'd spoken to over three hundred psychics during the time they'd known her. It is evident that Diana was deeply interested in the modern spiritual movement and on a number of occasions spoke about her own desire to develop spiritual healing powers.

In March 2003 Jane and I were approached by a Los Angeles–based film company and asked to conduct a television séance to contact the spirit of Princess Diana. They had heard about a mediumistic reading I had done for Chrissie F who was unknown to me but who had given Diana a colonic procedure. During the consultation, I had given a number of proofs that it actually was Diana communicating, even though initially I had no idea that it was the princess herself making the link. When I asked Diana for proof her identity, she mentioned two small silver-and-gold pillboxes, blue on top and of Romanov origin, that she'd given Chrissie as a gift. Diana told me the woman also had copies of letters from Elton John and Barbara Cartland in which Diana's name was mentioned. Afterward, the woman brought me photocopies of the letters and a photograph of the pillboxes.

The program Jane and I made with the American film company was titled *Spirit o Diana* and was screened around the world. According to the news reports, 30 million viewers saw a very different scenario from the times when I had to keep my gift secret!

Jane and I knew that this project would probably attract criticism from the skeptical press but it was also an important opportunity to present British mediumship to a world audience. And who better than Diana to help us? She was a mentor to many people for many different reasons, but what I loved most about her was that she was prepared to stick her neck out and speak the truth—and hang the consequences. Did Jane and I have the courage to follow her example? The program makers warned us that conducting a séance to speak to her spirit would certainly be controversial and no doubt attract criticism from the press. We were prepared to take them on.

The program was made in good taste and Jane and I took no fee for our services. Our immediate expenses were covered by an honorarium but not one penny went into our own pockets. We accepted the project out of admiration for Diana and a desire to bring British mediumship to a wider public. Throughout all of the sessions, rigorous safeguards were maintained by independent adjudicators to ensure that there was no possibility of cheating.

As a prelude to the upcoming teachings about the development of mediumship and to give you actual insights into how a medium works, I will explain a little about how we approached the séances.

The quest to connect to the spirit of Diana started in Paris, where Jane and I retraced the route she and Dodie Al Fayed took on the day of their death. I explained at the beginning of this book that when you set out on a quest that has spiritual significance strange synchronizations happen, and our quest to seek the spirit of Diana was accompanied by many odd twists of fate. One of the most remarkable coincidences happened on route to Paris: By sheer fluke, the driver of our limousine was the former personal chauffeur of Paris's other royal romantic exiles: King Edward VIII and Wallis Simpson.

Our first task with the TV crew was to use our psychic skills to see if we could get any clues about what had happened on that fateful journey in the early hours of Sunday morning, August 31, 1997 from The Ritz Hotel to the crash site at the Alma tunnel. We were using a form of psychometry to link into the vibrations of place and we made it clear to the viewers that this was a psychic skill and not, at that stage, a mediumistic link. We were taken along the journey from the back exit of the Ritz Hotel, across Paris to the Alma tunnel. On route we visited Dodie's flat on the Champs-Elysées, overlooking the Arch de Triomphe, and endeavored to tune in to its vibrations. Dodie's father, Mohammad Al Fayed, the owner of Harrods department store, also gave us permission to film in his flat in Mayfair, London, where again we described our impressions.

Both of us felt that the spirits of Diana and Dodie drew close to us as we visited the sites but, of course, at this stage nothing we said could be verified. Even our impressions while being driven through the Alma tunnel could not be confirmed or denied as there was already a vast amount written about this in the papers. Nonetheless, Jane and I were convinced that there was no conspiracy and that what had happened was simply a tragic accident. If indeed we had sensed Diana and Dodie near us at these times, then we believe that Diana's thoughts went out to her boys at the time of her death and Dodie's were for his father. Diana was not pregnant. I believe she forgives Charles.

Psychometry of an object or a place is not proof of a spirit communication. The next stage of the TV project was for Jane and me to give private consultations to a number of personal friends of the princess. These people would be able to confirm or deny any communication and verify any unique evidence that Diana spoke to us, thereby proving that it is not imagination. The venue was set as the Livery Hall of the Stationers Guild near St. Paul's Cathedral in London—the site of the wedding of Charles and Diana. This historic building had housed many royal events since its construction more than four hundred years ago.

To preserve the integrity of the program, only the head of research knew who would sit around the tables, and Jane and I remained at our hotel until our cars were instructed to bring us to the Livery Hall. Jane worked with the first group of people and I arrived later to work with the second group.

The producers understood that there were no guarantees that either of us would get anything through. You can't simply "summon" a spirit. I believe that about a million dollars was invested in the program, and the readings were, of course, pivotal to the success or failure of the venture. Not being paid relieved some of the pressure on Jane on me to "perform," but it was an awesome responsibility nonetheless.

Not everything Jane and I gave was correct, and one of the journalists (who referred to himself as "a shocking cynic") and a musician said later in the media that they were not convinced, despite having made positive testimonials on camera immediately after the filming. However, most of what we had to say for the more open-minded sitters contained very specific information that was highly personal and impossible to come by through research, etc. There was no way we could have known these things except through clairvoyance. Later in this chapter I will explain how the spirit communicates using a mix of clairvoyance, clairsentience, and clairaudience—seeing, hearing, and sensing.

When Diana drew close I became aware of her vivacious personality and of a somewhat mischievous mood as she took part in this highly contentious project. Turning to a young woman seated at the table, Diana passed me impressions of her continually writing. It turned out she was Louise Reid-Carr, Diana's personal assistant at the time of her death. Diana showed me the room where Louise used to work and I described to Louise how she used to stand by the window taking notes beneath a painting that Diana disliked. The earlier sitting with Chrissie F. flashed through my mind as Diana told me to say that Louise also had a close connection to the author Barbara Cartland, and Louise confirmed that Louise was related to the author. But what clinched it for Louise was when I related that when Diana used to go in to see her, the princess would go up to her, reach her hand into Louise's pocket, and say, "Let's have one of those sweets."

Louise admitted, with a smile, that she always kept a packet of pear drops in her pocket. I could hear Diana saying to me, "Tell her I want one of her sweets." The whole mood during Diana's communication was one of cheerfulness and fun, indicating that she wasn't in despair. I feel she hoped that by providing the proofs she had given to those present, her boys would also get the message that "Mummy's happy."

Interesting information also came through for a man, who I later discovered was called James Thurlow. Diana said, "Ask him about the menus. Tell him how I always tore them up. Tell him how I used to laugh about it and make it into a bit of fun." He looked astonished when I relayed this to him, and admitted that his job was to liaise with the chefs in the palace kitchens and discuss the menus for the day with the princess. I also said Diana had given him a special rolled parchment—a menu—when he retired, signed by her. He confirmed this—it was a hand-painted Italian rolled parchment, which he had framed and is now proudly hanging on his wall at home.

I said that when he used to go up to Diana's quarters, it was up an awkward spiral stone staircase and he'd often see her standing there frying eggs. He'd joke about how he'd cook all this food for her, only for Diana to go up to her room and fry eggs. James confirmed all this. I also told him that the princes weren't supposed to go up the spiral stone staircase, as it was the servants' entrance, but they did anyway and used to play marbles at the turn of the stair to the kitchen. I also related a story about how Diana had asked James to help in a frantic search on their hands and knees for a lost piece of jewelry—a funny event that James confirmed had happened.

It's the trivial things that most people wouldn't know that build up proof, and there is no doubt from watching the footage and his testimonial afterward that Mr. Thurlow was impressed. (The comment about the stairs and search for the jewelry was edited out of the first showing because I had a hacking cough that sent the sound meter off the scale but was referred to in James's testimonial at the end of the show and included in the second screening.)

I found out afterward that Jane had given equally impressive proof to her group. "Diana began to speak to me about AIDS, and I asked one of the women at the table, who I was drawn to at that point, why that might be," said Jane. "She told me she was HIV, and I later found out that she was Lynde Francis, founder of an HIV center in Zimbabwe. Diana also spoke of scar tissue on Lynde's leg that had nearly killed her. Lynde confirmed that she had had a skin graft after a snake bite in December, which had indeed nearly killed her. Diana also asked me to mention the earrings and say how glad she was to see Lynde wearing them again. Lynde explained that wearing the earrings was a big step, as she had been bed ridden for many months and had regretted being unable to wear them. Diana then showed me some children's clothes and pointed to an image of a baby wiping flies from its eyes. I told Lynde this, and she confirmed the night the princess had bought clothes out of her own money and given them to children at the orphanage Lynde ran.

"Next, I was drawn to a man who I was later told was Philip Godfrey-Night, who'd also met Diana and whose partner had died of AIDS. Diana wanted me to ask him about a plate of tea and cakes. He told me that when Diana met him at a hospice, she'd jokingly asked when she could come round for tea and cakes in his new kitchen. I also gave proof in that Diana was aware of a friend who was connected with the town of Brighton and who had died in his arms. She spoke of his good work with the terminally ill.

"While I felt privileged that Diana had shown me what really happened, I also felt emotionally exhausted. But it was clear to me her death was an accident, not a conspiracy. After that connection, I felt confident that the séance would be a success—as it proved to be. I know people will criticize us for having taken part in this program, but we wouldn't have done it if we didn't feel it was right. I felt Diana was happy with it and we couldn't have done it without her blessing."

APPLYING PSYCHIC AND MEDIUMISTIC SKILLS

During the Paris sessions to connect with Diana's spirit we were practicing a form of extended psychometry. Just as I have shown you how to read from an object, Jane and I were attempting to read vibrations contained in an environment. Now, under much less stressful circumstances than the scrutiny of TV, I intend to show you the skills that underlie a medium's work. I will also explain to you the differences between psychic and mediumistic work and give you a clear understanding of how to develop the skills of clairvoyance, clairaudience, and clairsentience.

Psychometry and the other techniques you have practiced help to develop your psychic skills. In time these methods will enable you to give accurate insights into a person's past and present situation. I believe that most open-minded people can develop these skills to some degree because we all retain these archaic ESP talents from before the advent of language. Working with others in a circle helps to reveal and enhance this latent potential.

Not everybody who joins my circle or development classes will become a medium. From what I have witnessed, mediumship appears to be something you are born with. The mediumistic gift may arise spontaneously during childhood—I used to see auras around people's head and often saw the spirit of my dead grandfather when I was a child. Throughout my teens this gift reoccurred in flashes of insight that were outside my control and which sometimes could be a little upsetting. It was only when I was shown how to sit for spirit and hone my talents that I was able to bring it under my control. If I had not had the opportunity to learn, the gift may have remained semi-dormant for the rest of my life, and all the exciting events, such as the Diana séances, never would have happened.

Perhaps you have the mediumistic gift. Perhaps you do not. You will only find out once you sit in circle. If it comes, then that is wonderful. If it doesn't ,that's fine too, for there are many other valid spiritual paths that will be shown to you during your development. And there will be at least one—maybe even more— route that will be perfect for you.

Some of my students have become good psychics, some have become healers, and some have become inspiring speakers. A few have become mediums. Hopefully all have benefited by becoming better people with a greater sensitivity and empathy for those in distress. Many students are happy working on a psychic level and may eventually become psychic counselors. Others take the fortune-telling route and apply their psychic skills to tarot-card reading and other forms of divination. These psychic ways of working are, of course, not mediumship, which is primarily to prove that the personality survives death.

Mediums Are Not Fortune Tellers

I am not against divination of the future so long as it involves genuine precognition and is not just arbitrary guesswork. Mediums do not predict the future during a consultation but may sometimes give advice about a direction to take. Nonetheless, this can be a bit of a gray area. For example, the great British medium Doris Stokes gave me a consultation twenty-five years ago and, although claiming not to be able to see the future, nonetheless named key people who would influence my life and foresaw events that are only now taking place. Her most astonishing insight was correctly naming my future wife (Jane Willis) and even the date we would meet (March 6th)!

On my website we do not allow predictions. Vi Kipling, my key helper, has succinctly summarized our policy relevant to anyone working with premonitions and prediction: "Mediums are not allowed to predict the future, and psychics who do so run the risk of feeding back to the sitter information picked up from the aura and which is usually the desired outcome the sitters wish for the problem posed to the psychic. For example, if the sitter desperately wants to remarry or receive a lot of money, this desire is exhibited in his or her auric energy field, a life force of light that surrounds every individual's body and is a reflection of each person's thoughts, feelings, emotions, etc. So the psychic tells the sitter what he or she wants to hear, which is not a good policy. It takes a very experienced psychic to override the demands made by the sitters and present to them a balanced view of their personality and any outcome to problems being experienced. It must be remembered that sitters *do not* wish to know their future or to have it predicted—that future could be very sad and nobody wants to hear that. Instead, they want to be told that everything is going to work out the way they wish. For a psychic to go down this road would be dishonest."

For more information about the moral and practical issues surrounding premonition, prophecy, and prediction, I invite you to read our website's British Clairvoyant Academy Code of Conduct. The code is a very simple set of common sense dos and don'ts that has now been adopted by hundreds of Internet practitioners and has become the Internet's foremost voluntary code of practice.

THE MEDIUM'S PATH

The truth is that few can develop mediumistic skills. And of those that have it, I have seen many give up for a variety of personal reasons. Even more frustrating are the fledglings who fly from the nest before they are ready or able to give quality links. They may get a few things right in circle and then immediately rush out and give private readings and demonstrations long before they are ready. They do themselves no favors, for their mediumship may remain at a substandard level for the rest of their lives and they will never know their true capabilities or what they could have achieved with patience. Just as dental students would not undertake deep root canal fillings until they are fully trained, so too mediums should not begin full practice until they have accomplished skills.

My own teacher, Peter Close, was a taskmaster who pushed us to greater and greater accuracy. We developed our mediumship with the same determination that a body builder develops his physique. I pushed myself to give a little more than my best every time I worked. This is one of the reasons I now am able to give such detailed proof and can take on TV challenges. For example, as well as giving the Christian name and surname of the spirit communicator, I can often relate information that cannot be claimed to be guesswork or researched from records. In a recent consultation I named the sitter's sister in spirit and explained how she died in a road accident. I told of how she had been buried in her wedding dress and was laid out clutching a china doll that held a distinctive blue rose. I was also able to quote the exact words of a letter she placed in the coffin, the contents of which were known only to the writer and now passed on to her dead sister.

I want new mediums to be inspired to give this level of proof, because when I die this next generation of mediums will be the people I will have to use to get a message to my loved ones. When I started out on the path, I never dreamed I'd be doing mediumship as a career nor would I be able to attain such a high degree of accuracy. It has happened because my teacher encouraged me, right from the start, to be tenacious about my mediumship, and this is what I want to pass on to you.

Never sit on your laurels, but continue to push yourselves to greater and greater accuracy. Never be satisfied to give a vague message. Be the one that proves beyond all doubt that mediums really can do what they say they can.

TYPES OF MENTAL MEDIUMSHIP

It is hard to describe exactly how mediumship works. You can be practicing for years and not get much, then suddenly it's there. It is just like riding a bike or surfing: Once you've cracked it and got the knack, it becomes automatic and easy. When the spirit communicator's thoughts resonate with the medium's subconscious mind an unobstructed flow of verifiable information comes through. To allow this to happen you have to discard that part of your mentality that wants analyze, rationalize, and shove everything into ordered boxes and instead embrace the holistic mind. In short, you "go with the flow."

Mental mediumship is the blending of a number of spiritual perceptions that work together to give the medium information about the spiritual communicator. (Note that we are talking here about *mental* mediumship, as opposed to *physical* mediumship, which builds the actual physical form of the spirit communicator.) If the medium is a clear channel then the spirit will be able to use a number of methods of inner communication to help prove the continuation of life after death. These are the following:

Clairvoyance. Literally "clear seeing," the ability to see spirit images. The medium's use of the word *clairvoyance* differs from the definition established by Joseph Banks Rhine, the father of parapsychology. A parapsychologist would describe clairvoyance as the power to see things that aren't available by the known senses and which aren't known by anyone else—for example, "remote viewing" which is the ability to view a remote location at a distance from the psychic.

For a medium the word *clairvoyance* has a slightly different meaning. Clairvoyance describes the visual information received from the spirit communicators. Working through the medium's aura, the spirit communicator will endeavor to impress his presence on the medium's mind. This could be described as a mental blending reminiscent of telepathy. When the medium receives these impressions his or her brain converts them into forms he or she can understand. In this case the information is "seen" in picture form.

Subjective clairvoyance is experienced in the mind's eye—that is, it is experienced inwardly. For example, the medium may have a mental picture of the communicator that he or she can "see" and describe. The details the medium may relay from this may provide a good visual description of the communicating spirit. The medium may also be shown other pictorial information and see images and movie-like impressions of scenes relevant to the communicator or the recipient. A personal memory and imagined images do not have the same clarity and detail as those received via clairvoyance. A clairvoyant vision of a communicating spirit person may show every wrinkle in excruciating detail, which adds to the evidence of survival. A description of a tattoo, birthmark, eye color, manicured fingernails, and so on can often provide more concrete proof to the recipient than the spirit person's name.

Some mediums experience what is called *objective clairvoyance,* seeing the communicating spirits as though they are reside in the physical world. In this instance, the spirit people are communicating through the medium's mind in the same way they do with subjective clairvoyance but the mental impressions appear to the medium to be part of his or her surroundings.

Clairaudience. Literally "clear hearing," the ability to receive spirit impressions in the form of sound. The spirit people do not speak to us in the usual sense. They transmit thoughts in the form of words through the aura to the subconscious of the medium. The medium's mind then builds this telepathically received information into words and sentences that are repeated to the sitter. The clairaudient medium has been compared to a person on the telephone who relays information to other people.

To give yourself insight into how clairaudience works try mentally reciting a verse or quotation. In your mind repeat each word as you think it. This is similar to inner experience of clairaudience—the
"voice" may appear distant or can be "heard" with clarity. With proper training the inner voice can become extremely clear so that all the medium need do is repeat exactly what is being said, without embellishment, to the sitter. For example, I have repeated a few sentences given from the spirit in the Urdu and Croatian languages, which I do not understand but to my utter astonishment I had spoken to my sitters (a phenomena known as xenoglossy). In most instances, if a foreign-language-speaking spirit communicates, I hear it in my native tongue of English. Telepathically projected thoughts from the spirit communicator are being made sense of by my subconscious, which I hear as my own language.

With *subjective clairaudience* there is a mental blending of the medium's thoughts with the spirit communicator. It is usually experienced as an inner voice. Using clairaudience the medium is able to give information such as the Christian name and surname of the spirit, the house number and street the spirit person used to live, his or her birth date and passing date. In fact there is unlimited information, facts, and advice that can be given in this way to guide the sitter or relieve the grief.

Sometimes a medium may experience *objective clairaudience*, in which the medium hears the voice as if it is being whispered in his or her ear or spoken in the room. In this form of mental communication the voice is heard only by the medium. That is why you sometimes see mediums talking as if they are in direct conversation with the spirit. This can look very impressive but the medium understands that in reality it is an objectified inner conversation that is taking place.

Clairsentience. Literally "clear sensing," the ability to sense spirit presence. The medium will be able to sense the bodily conditions, emotions, personality, and character of the communicator. I believe this is the easiest form of mediumship but also the most important, for clairsentience is usually always present during a communication. It is the string that threads together the pearls of clairaudience and clairvoyance.

Using clairsentience the medium will be able establish a great deal about the communicator. He or she will be able to sense if the communicator is a man, woman, or child. The medium can establish what physical ailments the communicating spirit had—including the cause of the bodily death, which is no doubt still foremost in the memory of the recipient. In addition, clairsentience can give information about the character, traits, and usual disposition of the spirit person. You may become aware if, for example, they were a stubborn person, a cheerful person, an intellectual person, and so on. All of this is vital information that is needed to establish a clear profile of the communicating spirit.

Objective clairsentience occurs when the mental impressions are superimposed on the medium's own body. For example, if the communicating spirit passed with a lung condition, I may feel a slight pressure on my chest. Sometimes these impressions can be very powerful. I recall having a sore throat for some time after describing the spirit of a young man who was beheaded by glass during a car accident. Objective clairsentience may cause the medium to unconsciously mimic the gestures, mannerisms, and facial expressions of the communicating spirit. I have found myself limping across the platform or speaking with a lisp, for example, when describing spirit people who had these conditions.

Clairsentience is an important part of mediumship because an accurate character profile can sometimes say far more than the hard facts about the deceased, such as names. Also important messages of love, feelings, and emotions are communicated through clairsentience.

HOW WOULD YOU LINK?

Imagine what it would be like if you were a spirit and were trying to communicate to your loved ones via a medium. You would soon realize that although the medium senses your thoughts, often the quality of the link changes and, like a bad telephone connection, loses its signal, becomes muffled, or lines get crossed. You would also notice that not many mediums have the ability to hear you (clairaudience) or may only hear words intermittently. How would you get your name across if the medium were spiritually deaf to what you say? You have to find other ways to impress his or her mind, such as using pictures, images, symbols, and sensations. Quite complicated information can be relayed in this way without using words at all.

The subconscious thoughts of the medium are influenced by the thoughts of the communicating spirit. The spirit communicator is aware of the medium's thoughts—like two computers sharing data over a network or the Internet. A medium opens his or her mind to allow the person in spirit to overshadow the medium's thoughts and also to give the spirit access to the medium's memories. This allows the spirit communicator to draw comparisons and make analogies from information the medium already knows in order to get the name across. The spirit person may, for example, highlight a memory about someone at school that the medium knew who had the same name as the spirit communicator. It would be like shouting out, "Hey my name is Fred. Just like the Fred you knew at school." A childhood memory of Fred would spring to the medium's mind and this may then be given as the spirit's name. In the same way, the spirit will draw many other comparisons to impress the medium's mind with similarities of stature, character, career, and so on. What appears to be the medium's memories are, in fact, the spirit communicator saying, "My character is just like this person you know" or "the events in my life were just like when this happened in your life" or "I died of an illness that was the same as this person you knew." Spirit communicators use the medium's own memories to make comparisons with themselves.

When this first happens you are likely to think that you are making it all up. Describing your own memories feels like cheating, but remember that you had these thoughts because the spirit communicator directed you to the associated memories. Students often complain that they cannot distinguish between what are their own thoughts and those given by the spirit. Overanalysis of this can sometimes trip them up.

Once the channel to spirit is open, every thought that comes to you during a demonstration is of significance. This is one more reason to "go with the flow" and give whatever comes to you without excessive analysis. (You would, of course, use your common sense and not make predictions, medical diagnosis, frightening remarks, and so on.)

For some of my students, realizing that the spirits are making use of their own personal memories as part of the communication is a milestone in their development. An excellent example of this occurred at one of my recent circles. We decided to work together with Chrissie, an invited guest of Christine's and someone that at that time none of us except Christine knew anything about. The session showed how each of the mediums worked differently to give an astonishingly detailed and evidential communication.

Phill kicked off by reading aloud a long list of facts about the guest's life that he had received in meditation and written down during the week before. He gave the exact place they had booked for their vacation as well as a profile of the recipient's grandfather, who had died in France during World War I. This technique is called advance clairvoyance, and is something I encourage everyone to practice for homework and bring with them to read out loud when we have a guest. The rest of the group worked specifically with clairvoyance, clairaudience, and clairsentience.

Sue "heard" the name of the communicator right away, while her partner, Daren, explained that he felt as if his hand had been cut off. Both had given accurate information, Sue using clairaudience and Daren using clairsentience. Meanwhile Steinar drew a simple portrait of one of the communicators and said that he had the urge to draw whales. "The place or the mammal?" I asked. In fact, the communicator had lived in Wales, the place. Steinar had been given a name by way of a picture, as I described earlier. For my own part, I connected with the spirit of a person called Charlie and his friend of short stature who Charlie showed as so short that he could not see over the bar. I have touched on only a few of large number of verified facts that came through, but what is of note here is that each of the practitioners used different forms of mediumship: clairvoyance, clairaudience, and clairsentience.

HANDS-ON WORK

My students have developed their skills in different ways and are encouraged to stamp their personality on their work. Some mediums I've watched are trained a little too well by the big teaching institutions and, although it is very important that mediumship is delivered with structure and clarity, they can sometimes appear a little robotic in their presentations. Others, who have not been trained, can be too gregarious and their presentations lack form, discipline, and quality. Mediumship is a science in that we are supplying verifiable facts, but it is also an art. Therefore we need to find a middle ground that makes it interesting to watch, allows our own personality to shine, and yet gives rock-solid proof that death is not the end.

Throughout this book I teach the development of mental mediumship, where the medium senses, sees, and hears the spirit communicator and repeats the information he or she is given. There are, of course, only two forms of mediumship: mental and physical, but there are phenomena within realm of *mental mediumship*. Some of these are *inspirational speaking*, in which the medium talks on a chosen spiritual subject and feels his words influenced by guiding spirit people; *trance speaking*, in which the spirit communicator talks directly through the medium using his or her voice box; *psychic art* inspired by the spirit helpers; and *spiritual healing*, in which the spirit guides aid with the work.

The second form of mediumship is *physical mediumship*, where an entranced medium, sitting in a darkened room, exudes a luminous, misty substance called ectoplasm. This mist solidifies into the faces, hands, and full form of the spirit communicator. An ectoplasmic spirit form is completely tangible and can be seen, heard, and touched by everyone present. Sometimes a rod of ectoplasm is formed that allows a spirit to talk through a "trumpet." Physical mediumship also includes the phenomena of *direct voice*, in which the spirit voice is heard independent of the medium; and also *transfiguration*, in which ectoplasm forms only over the entranced medium's face and a superimposed face of the spirit communicator is seen by the participants.

All of the above are advanced forms of the phenomena of mediumship and take many years to develop. They are not part of the objective of this book, which is aimed primarily at the novice and intermediate-level medium.

USING THE AURA IN MEDIUMSHIP

I am now going to teach you to link to the aura and give a psychic reading. I will then show you how to shift from psychic to mediumistic reading. In order to do this I need to teach you to sense and see the aura. For many students, seeing the aura can be a turning point in their development because it is tangible and objective. It give them faith in the fact that their gift is real and not just in their minds. However, not all mediums see the aura, so do not be disheartened if you discover that you do not have this form of psychic sight, for mental mediumship is an inner gift and it is ultimately love that makes it all work.

The aura can play an important part both in psychism and mediumship, as it links the medium to the sitter. Mediumship can also work from afar, when the sitter is not physically present, such as during a consultation by email, on the telephone, or in an Internet chat room. However, the sitter's physical presence makes it much easier for the medium to work because he or she is surrounded by so much beneficial energy. The medium's own powers are bolstered by a positive sitter and the auric energy of both parties will become a flow of power that fuels the session. In addition, the love being projected to and from those in the next life is also spiritual energy, and this more than anything else builds a bridge between the worlds.

The experiments that follow are best done in low lighting and without the distraction of candles or side lighting. If you are working during the evening the light coming in from outside through closed curtains may be enough. At my own group I use low red light for the aura-seeing experiments.

Sensing Aura

Step 1: The circle leader asks the members of the circle to relax and quiet their breath. He or she will then talk everyone through the experiment or can read aloud what follows.

Step 2: Rub your hands together vigorously so that you become sensitive to them. Now hold your hands about three feet apart with the palms facing each other. In a moment you will very slowly bring them together to the praying position and as you do this you are to concentrate on the sensations you feel.

Step 3: As you hold your palms apart, close your eyes and become aware of the aura energy surrounding your hands. Imagine that they are surrounded by a powerful force field. Now build the power of that force field. Experience the power surrounding your hands and feel it increasing in strength. Your hands are radiating energy. Notice how it is getting stronger and stronger.

Step 4: You will remember from your high school science lessons that like poles of magnets repel one another—they fly apart when brought together. Now imagine that the force field around your hands repel one another. They are like two opposing magnetic poles that force apart.

Step 5: Very slowly bring the palms of your hands closer together, so that there is now a gap of about one foot gap between them. Be aware of the force field surrounding the hands and between them. Notice how the energy reacts. Can you feel how the hands want to fly away from one another? Can you feel a tingling sensation as the hands get closer? The closer they get, the more the hands want to fly apart. It is like squeezing a partly inflated balloon.

Step 6: Now slowly bring the palms even closer together. As you do this feel the opposing force fields resisting each other. The closer the palms get the more your hands want to fly apart. Bring the palms closer still until now they are facing flat toward each other with just a fraction of an inch between them. Do not let them touch. Feel the huge resistance between them.

Step 7: Bring the hands fully together to the praying position. Relax and allow the sensations to subside.

When you have finished this experiment discuss the sensations you felt. It is likely that most people in the group sensed the feeling in their hands. When everyone is settled again, the group leader will talk everyone through a second experiment in the same way as before except this time the hands attract like the opposite poles of two magnets. They want to slap together as if being pulled together by a giant spring or giant elastic bands. Afterward discuss the sensations that were felt and how they differ from the first experiment.

The objective of this exercise is to show how we can influence the aura. These techniques of pushing and pulling the aura are used in Eastern self-defense teachings and particularly in tai chi. When we are in a threatening or an aggressive situation we unconsciously protect our auras and, conversely, in a secure situation our auras attract and we share energy. A sharing of auric energy may happen between people who care for each other and has a healing and restorative effect upon one another's health and well-being.

Extending Aura Sensing

This next exercise will help you to sense the aura of another person in a tangible way. Just as you felt repulsion and attraction between your hands, you can also use your hands to sense another person's aura and the feelings of pushing and pulling within the aura. You may also pick up other sensations, such as feelings of heat and cold as well as feelings of prickliness, sluggishness, heaviness, and so on. The sensations you experience when you run your hands through a person's aura and around their body will give you an indication of their spiritual, mental, and physical conditions.

You may become aware of the person's physical complaints but do not use this technique to make a medical diagnosis. If you are already a practicing healing medium, this method will alert you to the area of the aura and body requiring spiritual attention. If you are a member of a recognized healing federation, your code of conduct will advise you about these issues. The objective here is solely to learn a little more about how to sense the aura.

Step 1: The group leader pairs everyone. One person sits on a chair while the other stands beside him or her. The circle leader may use his or her own words or read aloud the steps below.

Step 2: The person standing will soon run his or her hands close to the body and through the whole aura of the person sitting. While this is happening, the person who is sitting will close his or her eyes and observe any feelings and sensations. Perhaps you can feel the hands moving through your aura. You may feel sensations of heat, cold, tingling, and so on as the hands move over your aura.

Step 3: The person standing may now run their hands around the body but not the head of the person sitting. As you do this you will note the sensations you feel from that person's aura. At first keep the hands a foot or two away from the person sitting and then gradually move the hands closer. At no point should you touch the other person.

Step 4: What sensations are you feeling as you slowly run your hands over your partner's aura? Can you feel similar pushing and pulling sensations as when you did the earlier experiment? Perhaps you can feel other sensations too? As your sensitivity increases so does your awareness of the sensations of the aura. In some places the aura may feel sluggish or energetic, at others spots there may be feelings of tension, balance, vitality, or weariness. Make a mental note of which are the sitter's strong areas and areas of weakness.

Step 5: Now move to the aura surrounding the head. Stand for a while with your eyes closed and your hands outstretched and palms facing inward to the head. What physical sensations do you feel in your hands? For example, a feeling of prickliness in the aura may indicate worries. Let your intuition give you the meaning. Does your intuition also tell you anything about the person's mental, emotional, and spiritual states of mind? Perhaps you also see images and pictures in your mind's eye. What do these symbols or images tell you about the sitter and his or her life at the moment? Within the person's aura are links to his or her inner self, with feelings, thoughts, memories, and so on. What are your psychic senses telling you about the person and his or her situation?

Step 6: Now move your fingers in close to the head and see what sensations you feel around the top of the head. This is the location of the crown chakra and the sensations you feel here as well as the thoughts that come to you now will give you insight into the person's spiritual ideals. Note any physical sensations as well as any mental impressions you receive. What do you sense about the sitter's personality, thoughts, emotions, and spiritual values?

Step 7: When a suitable time has passed, the leader stops the session and asks everyone to discuss the sensations you felt. First chat about the sensations you felt surrounding the body, but under no circumstances make a medical diagnosis. You may mention the areas where you felt the aura was weak or strong. You may, for example, say that you felt "hardness" to the aura around the knee but leave it to the recipient of the message to tell you that they have cartilage problems, or whatever. Avoid all talk of "holes in auras" or "leaking auras," as this is complete nonsense.

Step 8: Now discuss the feelings you had and any psychic impressions you felt around the head. What can you tell your teammate about their character, feelings, memories, situation, and so on. Tell them about things that have inspired them or are troubling them now. Describe their current circumstances without making alarmist statements or predictions.

Step 9: Finally, ask the recipient about their sensations. Perhaps they could feel where you had your hands most of the time or could feel if you had healing qualities.

Step 10: Now swap roles and try again.

This experiment has enabled you to give a psychic reading based upon the physical sensations and mental impressions gleaned from a volunteer's aura. When giving a reading, it is not appropriate to run your hands over a person's aura and certainly would not be possible when demonstrating to an audience. When I am first tuning in to a person, I sometimes sit with my palms on my lap and pointing to the person but this is certainly not essential. Linking to the aura remains a useful tool at the first stage of a reading. The technique become even more effective if you learn to see the aura.

Seeing the Aura

This next experiment is best done either in red light or low light.

Step 1: Hold your hands straight out in front of you. Look at the area surrounding the hands. Do not stare hard, you need to gaze rather than look. Can you see the aura surrounding the hands? It rarely appears as a bright light but is more like a gentle heat haze. Allow yourself to relax completely and gently watch the area around the hands for a while. You are not hunting to see the aura; a contemplative frame of mind works the best.

Step 2: Focus your attention on your hands but allow your eyes to focus on something further in front of you. If you are looking slightly downward you can focus on the floor. Shift your attention to the hands. They will appear out of focus but this will help you to get the knack of how to look. Can you see fuzziness around the hands?

Step 3: You are now going to increase the energy in the hands and focus it through the index fingers. Bring the index fingers of each hand toward one another until they are very close but not touching. As you did with the sensing exercises, feel the energy of attraction building. Look at the space between the fingertips. Can you see anything? The aura will appear between the fingers as a faint line of white light often with traces of blue and red. You may also see fine tiny lines of light right at the fingertips—like tiny spikes of light.

Step 4: When you move your fingers apart you will see that the light moves too. It is like having an elastic band of light between the fingers. Try moving the fingers in different ways: one toward you and one back, one up and one down, closer and then far apart. You can play with the light as if it is a piece of chewing gum caught between the tips of your two index fingers. I have seen students jerk backward in disbelief when suddenly they realize that they can see the aura with the same clarity as the normal world. See it once and its becomes easy to see every time. You'll be surprised you've never noticed it before.

Psychic Aura Reading

The techniques I have described are psychic techniques that can be used to read the aura of a person sitting in front of you. Just as you were able to sense and perhaps see the aura around your hands, you soon will start noticing the same effect around people's heads and body. You will see many colors and will be able to interpret what you see based upon what we already have learned about aura colors.

In addition, you will come to understand that the colors are influenced by a person's mood, character, thoughts, health, spirit, and general disposition. Recent troubles, hopes, and expectations may be revealed in their tones. Bright colors usually indicate a cheerful and healthy condition, whereas muddy colors or dark clouds may point to somber thoughts and possible ill health. There may be a predominance of a particular color that is with the person most of the time, but this may be overlaid with more dominant colors that are being caused by current emotions and thoughts. For example, if a person feels angry or physically charged their aura may be tinged with red.

Through the aura we connect spiritually to the person before us and are able to sense his or her thoughts, feelings, emotions, and memories. Even if we cannot see the aura we can still read it and can give a great deal of psychically received information. For example, we can make a good character assessment of the sitter and describe what has happened to him or her as well as know about the conditions currently surrounding that person. Naturally we have to be careful not to misunderstand the impressions we receive and feed back what we are getting in the wrong way. For example, if the person in front of us has just had a fight with his or her partner or has been concerned for some while about their relationship, then these thoughts will impregnate the area and we may sense them. A good aura reader may intuitively identify the problems and suggest some sensible ways of addressing the difficulty, but a bad reader may embroil their perceptions and predict a divorce or other extreme measures.

On a few occasions I have seen the colors of an aura manifest as patterns, shapes and forms. I have seen these tumbling out of the top of the sitter's head in a kaleidoscope of astonishingly beautiful shapes. However, most of the time when I link to the aura I see the colors and it is my own intuitive experiences that tell me all about the person. I have a feeling of "knowing" that transcends my normal rational thoughts.

When we are working as mediums to give proof of life after death we need to be careful not to mistake psychic content as proof of spirit communication. We could unwittingly be feeding back the sitter's memories of the spirit communicator that are being revealed through the aura. This would be telepathy—not mediumship. Aura reading is a useful steppingstone toward mediumship but remains a psychic skill. Mental mediumship is an inner process.

I will now illustrate how to move from a psychic reading to full mediumship.

MOVING TO MEDIUMISTIC READING

An aura reading session or a psychometry session can become the trigger for a full mediumistic reading, but I hope by now you appreciate the difference between this psychic work and mediumistic communication. If, for example, a student is doing psychometry and hits upon something that relates to someone in the spirit, I will allow the student to continue for a while but then will call a halt and ask that he or she put down the object.

Then the student will resume and work entirely with mediumship. If psychometry and mediumship are mixed then it is possible that the information is being obtained from the object's vibrations rather than the spirit communicator. Similarly, a good aura reading may reveal the sitter's memories about the deceased, but this can easily become muddled with what is being given from the spirit communicators. If this happens in class, and the student starts to get a spirit link while working, I allow him or her to continue working with the aura for a short while but then will ask the student to stop. I then encourage the student to look within for the information rather than to the sitter's aura, and then ask that he or she resume work and give an exclusively mediumistic reading based upon his or her own inner impressions.

While aura reading, psychometry, and other psychic techniques are a bridge to mediumship, they are not themselves mediumistic communication. I use many psychic methods to get my students started but eventually a time comes when they learn they need to work entirely with mediumship.

Mediumistic Linking

For the first year or so I develop my students' psychic skills as a prelude to mediumship. If mediumship happens spontaneously during a psychic reading, I encourage those students in ways I have just described, and it is a sign that some of them may be ready to work exclusively as mediums. It is at this stage that I introduce the extended sitting-for-spirit period I about setting up a circle.

Once the circle has had the opening sessions and meditation, the group leader calls everyone back to normal awareness and asks them to return to the relaxed meditative state of mind to sit for spirit. For these sessions we usually invite a guest to work with but, alternatively, the members of the group can work on one another. A point will come when you will need a guest, because over time you will have gotten to know a little too much about one another. I will assume that you have a guest for this next experiment.

Step 1: Open the communication. The link with spirit is made through the power of love. During the period you are sitting for spirit you may feel the presence of people you know in the spirit draw close or you may see colored lights and visual images and feel the closeness of your guides. You will feel calm and peaceful within. During this "meditation" you will also become aware of the guest's loved ones.

Step 2: Build a rapport. Don't expect to suddenly see spirit forms or hear voices. The bridge between the two worlds is built slowly. Mentally note the things you see and feel and any impressions you get. A name may come to mind or you may feel the closeness of someone who wants to communicate. Use your inner dialogue to ask the spirit people about themselves. Ask an inner question. Wait for an inner answer. At this stage you do not know if the answer is coming from your own thoughts or not but soon you will be able to ask the guest for verification.

Step 3: Deepen the communication. The spirit people will be aware that you are attempting to develop mediumship and will draw close to help. They will understand the level of your development and won't frighten you or push you into a trance. Mediums are always in control. A mental conversation is held with the spirit person. So ask questions inwardly and most importantly listen to the reply. The more you interfere with the incoming impressions the more distorted your evidence becomes. Let the spirit people do the work but push the communicator to give evidence. The guides will bring the communicator forward but you must encourage them to speak.

Step 4: Remember the communication. When the group leader calls everyone back to normal awareness all of the circle's sitters will write down their impressions in their notebook or spiritual diary. Include absolutely everything you can, even those things that appear to be silly, trivial, or unimportant. What did you see, hear, and feel during the session?

Step 5: Each person in turn reads out what information and impressions he or she has been given and the guest gives verification or otherwise. Sometimes, if particularly good information has been given by some of the group, I will ask them to have a try at mediumship without notes. Using methods that I will soon describe, they give further details about the communicator. Occasionally I will open the floor to all of the circle members and we will simultaneously work together to give proof from one or a number of spirit communicators. The details you receive through a pure spirit link while sitting for spirit and before working with the guest can be very convincing proof of survival because it is not influenced by the sitter's facial expressions, tone of voice, or body posture.

I use this same procedure when demonstrating mediumship on my Internet chat room demonstration evenings, which are usually packed to capacity with visitors. While the other mediums are demonstrating or giving a discourse I spend time sitting for spirit in front of my PC monitor. When I come out of the meditation I use my notes as the basis for my reading and type them into the chat applet. The information I type about the spirit communicator usually finds its target.

It is extraordinary how my mediumistic colleagues and I are able to give so much proof without knowing anything about the people in the rooms. The medium does not know if the recipient is male or female, old or young, or even which country he or she is from. All we have is a chat name. One recent demonstration I gave was from a spirit man named Charlie, who said he was a body builder in life. He showed himself drinking a special milkshake straight from the blender. He then relayed to me some funny stories that I passed on to the recipient—such as the time he used the family cats as dumb bells and another incident in which he hammered a wooden sign onto the door that said "The Flintstones." The recipient was in tears because all these unusual facts proved to her that her brother had survived death.

Verifiable evidence that comes in advance like this is hard for the skeptics to counter. Certainly with such unusual evidence the recipient is not making the information fit and there is absolutely no way the medium could watch the sitter's eye movements, body posture, voice tone, facial expression, and so on

Developing Your Mediumistic Link

A time will come when you feel confident enough to directly make a spirit link. When you work as a medium don't try to mimic other mediums—even if they are celebrities. Be yourself. Every medium is different and there are as many ways of working as there are different human personalities. The spirit guides will help you to develop your own style but there are a few basic ways to establish a clear communication that can act as a framework for your work:

First you need to "link" to your sitter. Ask him or her to say a few words, as some mediums believe that the sound of the voice establishes a vibration link between the sitter and medium. In the early stages of your mediumship you may begin working at a psychic level and then use this as a way to progress to full mediumship. Begin by telling the sitter a few things about their own personality, present life, and past. As the psychic bond between you builds, look to your inner impressions and ask in your mind for the spirit people to give you some information about themselves. Ask questions inwardly and, most important, listen to the reply. The more you interfere with the incoming impressions the more distorted your evidence becomes.

Let the spirit people do the work but push the communicator to give evidence. The guides will bring the communicator forward but you must encourage them to speak.

Here are some steps to follow to build a psychic bridge between the two worlds. As you progress you will establish your own way of working, but whatever your method try to establish structure to your communication.

Step 1: Ask the spirit communicator what sex they are. Relay your information to your sitter. For example: "I have a lady with me."

Step 2: Ask the spirit communicator to show you their body size and again say what you feel. For example: "It's a big, cuddly lady."

Step 3: Now identify if the communicating spirit is family, friend, or acquaintance. Ask the question in your mind and the spirit will impress you with the feelings. For example you may say: "This is a family member. I feel a motherly vibration. I believe I'm with your grandmother on your mother's side of the family."

Step 4: You have now established the identity of the spirit communicator and the recipient will be able to connect the forthcoming facts to that person.

Step 5: People always remember how their loved one passed, and you can use clairsentience to discover this information. Ask the spirit about his or her last illness and how he or she passed over. Was it a quick death, such as by a heart attack? Was it an accident? Or was it slow, such as with bone cancer or a degenerative illness? You may sense the illnesses throughout the spirit's life as well as specific illnesses. The information will be given to you. You may then say something like: "This lady suffered with her back throughout her life. She had long-term stomach problems but she passed quickly with a heart attack." You will feel the communicators earthly physical conditions overlaid over your own body and more information may come to you as you are talking. If you ever feel uncomfortable, ask the spirit communicator to take the condition away. Of course, the spirit person no longer suffers as he or she did on earth—and you may point this out in your messages—but the conditions of their passing are a powerful part of the proof.

Step 6: Now ask the spirit communicator about his or her personality and character traits. Was he or she a happy person? Stubborn or easygoing? Did he or she have any unusual personality quirks? You will experience the spirit communicator's qualities, thoughts, and feelings in your own thoughts. You may say to the sitter something like: "Your grandmother could really dig her heals in. She was bossy and liked to push your grandfather around." Tell the sitter as many things as you can about their grandmother's personality. Build a character profile in the same way you did in chapter 4, on psychometry. This time you are not reading an object or a flower, you are reading a real spirit person.

So far you have been using mainly the psychic gift of clairsentience to describe the spirit communicator. You've used it to confirm the sex, bodily form, illnesses, and personality of the spirit person. You've applied similar intuitive skills to those you practiced on through psychometry and aura reading. You have also learned to listen to your inner impressions and have asked questions directed to the spirit. The next step is to engage clairvoyance—to see pictures and images.

Step 7: Ask the spirit communicator to impress you with images and visions. Some mediums experience this as coming through the third-eye chakra located on the forehead. Relay what you see. Again don't censor your thoughts. For example: "I see a lion." The sitter looks perplexed. "A red lion. Did she work at a pub called the Red Lion?" The images have a meaning. At first you may misunderstand what you are getting or muddle spirit's impressions with your own thoughts. Continue asking the spirit communicator to expand the image and you'll understand the message they are trying to convey. Sometimes your subconscious may turn the spirits thoughts into symbols.

Step 8: If a phrase, name, or sentence is on your mind, speak it. When you are working as a medium most of the thoughts that pop into your head are given to you by the spirit communicator or by your spirit guides. It's no good saying afterward, "Oh, I was going to say that"—you're too late. There may also be occasions when you get only part of the message being given to you, but a little perseverance may help you to flesh it out. For example, you may say: "I hear the place name San Diego." The sitter says she or he has no connection with California. "No it's not San Diego, it's the name Diego. Do you understand the Christian name Diego?" the medium may ask the sitter. The sitter may then understand this as their dead friend's name. People are often not very helpful when you give readings and you have to spell it out for them!

At first clairaudience—hearing the spirit—comes slowly. Although the "voice" may appear to come from the ear, in reality it comes from the mind. Initially you may not get all the names right. Clairaudience is an advanced way of working within mental mediumship and, in my opinion, may be inherently difficult to achieve because mediumship uses the nonverbal right side of the brain. If I get the name wrong, I generally will not try a second time. A vague "I've got a J name with me" is poor mediumship, as is throwing out a list of common names. Persevere and the names will come because the information you are receiving from spirit is correct. All is clear, only you are clouded.

7 SPIRITUAL INVESTIGATIONS AND GHOST HUNTS

"Let's put the fun back into fundamentalism."
—Anonymous

The first Spiritualist circles since the establishment of the movement in 1848 sat most weekday evenings over many years with the result that extraordinary miracles had time to manifest at séances and circles. Physical phenomena such as apports (objects teleported to the séance), discarnate voices, levitation, materializations, and ectoplasm were widespread. Today these phenomena have all but disappeared because modern circles cannot give the level of dedication required for this degree of spirit manifestation. Life today is so fast-paced and we have many more commitments and distractions than did the Victorian pioneers of mediumship.

If you wish to develop mediumship, you need to sit regularly and over a number of years. At the time of this writing I have been running my circle for over fifteen years, and I am pleased to say that I am still able to maintain my students' interest. I recognize that we all need a degree of change and new stimuli and I address this by introducing a variety of unusual techniques and settings.

Discovering mediumship is a joyful experience that can be both fun and serious. We often associate spirituality, particularly in the guise of religion, with long faces, heavy books, and somber clothes or, at the other extreme, as a happy affair with followers clapping, jumping around, or fainting from religious fervor. Sensible spiritual seekers find a middle road: They are serious in their intent but their heart is filled with compassion and cheerfulness. I believe that developing spirituality can be inspiring—and entertaining.

I like to introduce variety to what we do and this includes working, whenever possible, in new environments. It is stimulating to meet new people and to discover new places. My circle is often on the move, visiting other groups, circles, and spiritual organizations to demonstrate our skills and to learn and share ideas. One of our most popular and enjoyable pursuits is walking and talking.

SPIRITUAL WALKS

Research has shown that walking has many therapeutic benefits: It improves our health, sharpens the perceptions, even heightens our intelligence, and if done at a beautiful natural location awakens our sense of spirituality. This is why I take my circle rambling through the countryside once a week. I believe that a medium needs to pay particular attention to his health in general, because mediumship can be exhausting work and may sometimes draw too much on our auras reserves of prana and may eventually result in illness.

True, you get fit by walking, but there are many other benefits. It is rewarding to swap stories and discuss spiritual ideas, and the interest that comes from endlessly changing landscapes and the moods of the weather will sharpen perceptions. The scent of the earth in a pine forest after rain, the vista of clouds piled one on top of the other in a blue sky, and the thrill that comes when mist clears from the mountains to reveal their magnificence are pleasures that bring us back to our spiritual roots. When we are with nature we are surrounded by millions of years of unhurried evolution, and I am reminded of the people of the past who walked the same paths and, like us, talked and wondered about the reason we have been placed here. I am reminded that my life is just a small part of a much bigger picture. Walking in places of beauty liberates the emotions and awakens the five senses—and perhaps the sixth sense too.

In India it is believed that hatha yoga prepares the body for the changes in the aura that come with the advanced meditation techniques. I practice yoga but also have taken up swimming to improve my health through cardiovascular exercise. I have noticed a marked improvement not only in my vitality but also in my spiritual work. For example, I do an annual event for a corporate client that sees me doing a great number of one-on-one readings during the day. Normally after eight hours of nonstop reading sessions and a long journey to London and back I am exhausted to the point that I can hardly stand up and have even experienced double vision when I am so tired! Since I began swimming—with a rigorous aquatic session just prior to the event—I am not only able to sustain a high level of quality mediumship throughout the day but an able to remain active when I get home. Instead of collapsing like a broken man onto the sofa, I'm up for taking Jane out late-night shopping—one of the most exhausting tasks known to man.

While walking we avoid talk of money, relationships, TV, and other mundane things and instead focus on creative and inspirational discussions. We talk about nature, philosophy, the meaning of existence, the purpose of mediumship, and so on. Sometimes our walks resemble a pilgrimage, except our spiritual quest has no destination because for us the journey is more important than the goal.

When the BBC accompanied us to film one of our walks it gave us the opportunity to express our ideas about modern spirituality. The resulting program showed how we use this time to discuss mediumistic technique, encourage one another, and plan our presentation. On this occasion in particular I wanted to empower Daren, who was to do his first demonstration with Jane and me in a theater. Walking is an informal opportunity to talk about ideas and answer questions from the students, leaving the time spent in circle for practice and application. During our walks we can talk about the progress we are making individually and as a group and how we can use our knowledge to make a difference in the real world. The time spent walking, and sometimes also being perilously lost in thicket, builds a team spirit and further strengthens the fellowship of the circle.

Walks can also be used to practice our psychic skills, so we often set a course to places of mystical significance or that have an intriguing history. We plan visits to historical sites, haunted locations, or simply choose to walk at beautiful places where the energy of nature is high. At these places I teach my group to "tune in," as they have learned with psychometry, to the vibrations and residual energy recorded in the fabric of the environment.

I am fortunate living in Hampshire, England, where we can ramble beside many historical and ancient megalithic sites. Close to my home is Winchester, once the capital of Wessex, England; to the northwest are the ancient standing stones of Stonehenge, Woodhenge, and Avebury. These ancient sites are claimed to radiate earth energies that bring fertility to the land. It is believed that people who are receptive or who have clairvoyant awareness can sense this earth energy. At these places we sometimes meditate and attune ourselves to the vibrations, for we claim that just as we can read the past from an object when we do psychometry, so too can we tune in to the residual energy of a landscape.

EARTH DOWSING

In the 1924 the Herefordshire businessman and amateur archaeologist Alfred Watkins published a book called *The Old Straight Track*, which was responsible for an explosion of interest in dowsing and, in particular, dowsing for earth energies. Watkins noticed from maps and from his rides in the countryside that some ancient sites, such as stone circles, standing stones, churches built on ancient sites, and tumuli (ancient burial mounds) fell into an alignment. He originally thought these lines to be old traders' routes and named them *leys*—an Anglo-Saxon word for cleared glade—a term he borrowed from the archaeological writer J. P. Williams-Freeman who also had noticed similar correlations.

Of particular interest, was the fact that many of these leys formed "tracks" that corresponded with the path of the stars, planets, and sun. Many authors subsequently argued that ley lines pointed to a hidden history that was written into the geometry of ancient sites around the world. Ley lines, they claimed, are a network of interconnecting energy fields that were understood by the ancients to be beneficial to life. It was theorized by famous dowsers such as archaeologist Tom C. Lethbridge, who died in 1971, that the human body is a sort of antenna that is attuned to the influences of nature and will, for example, instinctively know the proximity of underground water and other hidden things. The ancients were attuned to this intuitive knowledge and applied it to harness nature by building their standing stones at places they believed would influence the earth energy. Megalithic monuments were acupuncture points that benefited the flow of the planet's life force and boosted its fertility. John Michel, in his book *View over Atlantis*, argued that this ancient geometry of the leys and the astrological correspondences of ancient standing stones point to a lost knowledge with its roots in the legendary civilization of Atlantis.

I believe some of these ideas are nonsense, but it is certainly the case that my group and I do sense unusual energies at these places and that dowsing appears to respond to these energies. There is, of course, a danger of allowing fantasy to rush in to fill in the vacuum left by the absence of empirical facts about prehistory, so I encourage a measured approach to anything we may discover. Psychically retrieved information needs to be qualified by historical facts, though few clairvoyants would deny there is something intriguing about the energies we believe we sense at these mysterious places.

Dowsing for ley lines is not a mediumistic gift. My objective with these outings, and particularly with psychic archaeology, is to refine my students' psychometry skills, which, as you have read, is a clairsentient pathway toward mediumship. Just as psychometry unlocks the history of an object, so too dowsing and consciously attuning oneself to nature's energy put us in touch with the vibrations of the earth and its history. According to Eastern philosophy, the prana life force is present in everything. I believe it to be a mycelium of energy that connects everything to everything else—including this world with the next.

How to Dowse

Divining rods are easy to use and can be employed for finding water or other hidden substances. The best way to learn how to dowse is to go out and try it. Dowsing rods can be purchased on the Internet or you can easily make them yourself from two pieces of coat hanger wire bent about a third of the length into a right angle and slipped into two plastic tubes that allow them to swing from side to side.

Step 1: Keep your arms by your side and relax. Take a rod in each hand, holding them loosely by the sleeve so that the metal rod moves freely.

Step 2: Bring your arms up so the rods are horizontal and about one foot apart (30.5cm) They should be held parallel to each other and facing forward.

Step 3: Walk forward holding the rods in this position as you focus your attention on the object you are searching for. They will cross each other when you walk over water or over the hidden source you are looking for.

Step 4: Once you have mastered the rods over a short distance you can widen your search. Mark the spots when the rods react and try approaching your markers from different angles. Keep marking the spots where the rods cross to identify your find. Perhaps the markers will make a line suggesting that you have found a hidden pipe or an underground stream.

Step 5: In the same way, the rods can be used to seek places of high earth energy or to track the course of a ley line. The rods will respond to whatever object you hold in your mind, whether it is water, gold, oil, lost objects, a historic site, or a ley line.

Dowsing is a fun way to become attuned to the energy of a place and gives you empirical proof that these energies are real. You may also practice map dowsing with pendulums during circle. Further techniques are posted on my website www.psychics.co.uk.

GHOST HUNTS

Just as the energy of a place can be sensed by a medium with psychometry skills, so too can the energy vibrations retained in buildings. Homes, churches, theaters, and so on all have their own special atmosphere that can be felt by anyone who is clairvoyantly sensitive. My circle can learn a great deal from tuning in to the vibrations associated with buildings, and what better destination for our experimental outings than to visit somewhere that is haunted?

I have received many interesting letters and emails about ghosts and haunted houses through my newspaper columns, but unfortunately most of these relate events that had happened in the past. I was very pleased, therefore, when a reader called to say that poltergeist and other phenomena were active in his home as we spoke. He lived about an hour's drive from me and, if I hurried, I could experience it firsthand. I took his address and got in my car.

The man was intelligent, of reasonable disposition, and convincing. He took me to the upstairs bedroom where he said it was all happening. He explained that the ghosts appeared out of nowhere and looked like tiny manikins, usually only a few inches high and sometimes had an insect like appearance. "There's one!" he yelled pointing underneath the bed. Immediately we both fell to the floor and peered beneath the bed. "Can you see them? Look, that one's playing a tuba. Look, look! There's a whole band marching. They have uniforms!"

As I lay there on this stranger's bedroom floor looking for an imaginary brass band I made a decision. Next time I would not be quite so enthusiastic—and I certainly would learn much more about mental illness. In the majority of paranormal reports there is usually a reasonable explanation for the phenomena or a psychological cause at its heart. Often most supposed "malevolent spirits" or "possessions" can be attributed to the early stages of schizophrenia, and it is understandable that troubled people turn to mediums at the onset of hearing threatening voices. They are unlikely to recognize that these convincing hallucinations are the result of a medical condition. I have read enough psychiatry to recognize schizophrenic behavior and my wife, Jane, was once a fully trained psychiatric nurse.

I would suggest that before you study ghosts and possession you study a little psychology. In particular read up on latent schizophrenia, narcolepsy, waking dreams, and sleep paralysis, as these conditions are mistakenly believed to have a paranormal cause by amateur ghost hunters. Then if a supposed paranormal case presents itself, you will recognize if it has a psychological cause and know where to direct the person to get qualified help. Be discrete and remember that there is still a great deal of stigma and ignorance associated with mental illness but also that in recent years great advances have been made to treat the condition.

One of my best friends from school was in later years diagnosed as schizophrenic, and I noticed that he had genuine ESP powers and I saw objects around him move when he project mental energy. Personality disorders require treatment by a specialist but it saddens me when real paranormal powers are disregarded. I recall the time a psychiatrist who knew of my interest in these things asked me to accompany her to the home of one of her patients to investigate an alleged haunting. When we stepped into the hall a white mist fingered its way across the floor, under our feet, and out the front door. The psychiatrist went as white as a porcelain doll, and I am sure she now listens a little more closely to her patient's claims.

When I take my circle to investigate haunted places I am careful to select venues where there has been reported activity over a period of time rather than recent activity that surrounds just one individual or family. The objective of these outings is to distinguish between residual energy and a conscious spirit. It also serves as important training for the future if ever the students are approached to deal with this type of phenomena.

One of the most exciting expeditions we undertook was with the BBC's camera crew in tow. They were there to film us tracking ghosts as part of a documentary about my psychic training program. The crew was told the history of the location but we were to be kept in the dark until breakfast on the morning we were to leave. I had hired a mini bus and drove the group to the location, which was told to us only moments before setting off, as a safeguard to prevent any of us from looking up the venue in books or on the Internet.

The map reference we were given took us to a manor house called Athelhampton House in Dorset, England—close to the historic village of

Tolpuddle, where the first-ever trade unionists were arrested, tried, and punished. I know now that Athelhampton House has a long and checkered history and that many frightening ghosts are said to haunt it. We were to conduct a circle-*cum*-séance and stay the night.

Approaching the manor at night made it look like a very scary place, with a dark entrance that looked like a menacing portal to Hell. "That's your room there," said the producer, pointing up at a gothic tower with sinister church widows. It was clearly going to be a disquieting night's sleep for Jane and me. Christine and her sister, Haley, were the most nervous of our group and one of the crew let it slip that they used to hang people in the room that was to be their bedroom. Although it is my job to reassure people, I couldn't help adding that my guess was that they probably laid out the corpses exactly where Christine and Haley would be lying. If either sensed a ghost it would most probably feel like the ethereal shell of a rotting corpse superimposed over her own body. (I believe Christine and Haley stayed up all night, because Jane and I heard their blood-curdling screams intermittently during the night

A circle can learn from haunted houses about the vibrations and energies that are "recorded" into the environment. To help us with this we conducted a circle in the main hall, in front of a roaring log fire. Our hostess, the mistress of the house, gave us a number of artifacts belonging to former occupants, which we read using our psychometry skills. The owner was able to verify that we were describing a number of dead residents, some of whom were said to still haunt the halls, rooms, and twisting corridors.

With confirmation that we were now linked to the vibrations of the former occupants, we could now extend our sensitivity to include the vibrations of the house in general. What could we discover about its history and occupants? And most importantly for the owners, were there any ghosts that they need worry about?

One area that we were drawn to was the landing that adjoined the wing where we were to sleep. Beneath a painting of an Elizabethan woman I saw and described the gray figure of a woman who, I sensed, moved across the corridor, through our bedroom, and into the small chapel that adjoined our bedroom. This was also sensed by others in the circle and confirmed by our hostess as having been seen many times before. Jane reassured her that these things would not be harmful in any way to her young family. Indeed, Jane gave verifiable and comforting proof from a male relative and child who communicated to reaffirm this.

PSYCHIC SCHOOL

As the exploration of the house continued our sensitivity to the residual vibrations increased. Wandering through a comparatively modern part of the house I was suddenly and quite forcibly impressed by the image of a raging fire. My throat tightened as I perceived choking smoke—a sensation simultaneously experienced by Daren. Steinar, who was standing with us, stumbled forward, expressing that he felt someone push him. We explained our impressions to our hostess, who confirmed that a fire had started exactly where we said and that sometimes people see a figure standing there—as if giving a warning or raising the alarm. Sometimes people walking through this area had a feeling that an invisible hand is giving them a hard shove.

Later that night, while chatting around the fire, Christine asked about orbs and whether our cameras were likely to catch any. Orbs are rings of light that sometimes appear on film and are claimed by some to be photographic proof of the presence of spirit energies. Christine had touched a sore spot. There had been so much silly talk on the website chat rooms about orbs recently that I was now quite dismissive of them. I get sent hundreds of supposed orb pictures via my website and in my opinion it is dust, lens flair, processing flaws, etc. It seemed to me that every blob of light on a flawed camera was interpreted as something supernatural. Soon I was on my high horse and I launched into my usual discourse about what a load of rubbish all this was. We all felt the temperature in the room drop like a stone. Sensing this was an important moment Daren took a photograph. Next to my ear was an orb of light. Time to eat my hat.

Most interesting of all were the secret passageways. We soon used our psychic skills and a bit of knocking on walls to discovered the hidden doors. Daren, Phill, Jane, and I descended the tight spiral stairway into the darkness of the secret passageway and hidden chamber. We tuned in. All of us felt that an animal was important and that there was something strange about this animal. We agreed there were a lot of thoughts in the atmosphere here about animals but whether it was a ghost or not was questionable. Our conclusion was that the secret passageway had been the favorite place of the family pet—probably an Alsatian dog—and that over the years this had been exaggerated into a tall tale about the lair of a mysterious animal ghost.

A great deal of verified information was picked up from all of us about the residual psychic energy of the building, but despite the spooky appearance of the house we concluded it was not haunted. There were certainly some strange energies sensed, and among us we gave an accurate description of the house's past and its former occupants, but was it haunted by a ghost?

Probably not. We all could sleep easy that night even though all the lights would now have to be dimmed to save power and to adhere to fire regulations. Unfortunately Christine and Haley had already wandered off down the lonely corridor to their bedroom in the other wing of the house before we could explain that we had found no active entities in the house.

The next morning Christine and Haley reappeared from the lonely tower looking bleary-eyed from a sleepless night. At the base of their bed was a white Victorian crib which, it was said, would rock by itself when spirits were present. I believe it creaked a few times during the night, sending Christine and Haley into a panic which of course accounted for the screams Jane and heard at the dead of night. Over breakfast our host and hostess explained how much we had gotten right. The mistress of the house was impressed because there was clearly no cheating going on. On another occasion, for another TV program, she was upset to see the medium repeat a number of red herrings from the website, including a yarn about a monkey ghost that had been made up one evening for a joke around the dinner table. It was now stated as fact on their website but was of course just a story.

Ghosts

Most supposed haunted houses have about as many ghosts as my granddad's pocket watch. The example I have given shows how sensing residual energy is similar in many ways to using psychometry to read an object's past. What we experience at haunted houses are the imprints left in the earth's energy field. Some scientists accept that brain waves emit an electrical field that can effect and leave a trace on the surroundings. This ethereal impression can be compared to the way a camera records a scene or the chemicals on photographic paper produce an image when exposed to light. A clairvoyant is aware of these thought waves that project through the aura and infuse into the environment. Ancient places are saturated in the recorded thought energies of generations of visitors.

Powerful emotions such as fear, hate, and anger leave powerful impressions in the surroundings. In chapter 4, I pointed out that sensitivity to these things may be a pre-language survival mechanism that warned our more sensitive ancestors of places that were dangerous. I believe that the recorded emotions theory extends to ghosts. Ghosts may be the manifestations of human emotions that have been projected during traumatic events. Events involving grisly deaths, prolonged tragic circumstances, and drama are likely to leave behind an imprint. Therefore, a ghost is like a photographic record that is occasionally visible to sensitive people. It is seen like a film clip from the past, sometimes with the same scene repeating in the same spot. What is seen is certainly not a conscious spirit trapped in a time warp and repeating the same task for eternity. It is the energy of history.

Many people become very frightened when they see a ghost but in actuality there is no cause for alarm. The real people, their spirit selves, have moved on long ago into the world of the afterlife.

SPIRIT ENTITIES

Spiritualists believe that at the time of death the spirit leaves the physical body and manifests in an *etheric* body—also sometimes called the subtle body or body of light. The etheric body enables the continuation of the spirit and, with it, the persistence of our memories, feelings, identity, and consciousness. At death we let go of the confinements of the physical body and in the vehicle of the etheric body we effortlessly soar into the infinitesimally beautiful world of the beyond.

Sometimes at the time of death there remains unfinished business of great importance and the spirit person may urgently want to contact loved ones on earth. Many of the communications that non-mediumistic people receive come just days after a passing. We do not know for certain why this is the case but perhaps during this time the spirit's energy is different in some way to give it the chance of one last communication before moving on. Usually when a spirit appears to a loved one it is for the purpose of saying a silent goodbye or to let their loved ones know they have survived.

A spirit entity is not a ghost, the difference being that a spirit is conscious, whereas a ghost is an unconscious memory imprinted onto a specific place. A ghost's behavior never varies, whereas a spirit may manifest at different times and impart a variety of information. You will probably recognize the spirit form of someone you love, whereas a ghost is simply a manifestation of someone else's experiences.

Certainly there are occasions when a conscious spirit appears to haunt a specific place. For example, Spiritualism was founded soon after the sisters Margaretta and Kate Fox purported in 1848 that the strange rapping that surrounded them came from the spirit of a dead tinker named Charles Haynes, whose remains were later discovered buried in the basement of their house in Hydesville, New York. There are those who believe that sometimes spirits fall asleep or become trapped on the earth plane either because they do not know they are dead or are helplessly clinging to their former lives. I have experienced a number of rare instances where we have encountered a conscious earth-bound spirit, though I believe even this experience could be explained by the projected fear energy of a living person.

It is advisable to take a common-sense approach and trust your own experiences as the measure of what is real and what is not. You may read many strange ideas that are written as facts but are, in reality, written by people who have no mediumistic ability or experience of spirit. And not all mediums speak sense you know!

I advise my students to keep their feet on the ground and not to get carried away with fantasy. When you take a measured and stable approach to these issues you soon come to realize that there is nothing whatsoever to be frightened of with regard to ghosts and spirits.

8 ADVANCED TECHNIQUES

"Spirit guides can and do perform kindly offices for those on earth, but benefit can only be received on the condition that we allow them to become our teachers, not our masters, that we accept them as companions and not Gods to be worshiped."
—Andrew Jackson Davis (Spiritualist pioneer)

The medium stood solemnly on the rostrum of the Spiritualist church and with closed eyes said in a silly Chinese accent, "Greetings from the spirit world." This was one of Jane and my favorite mediums because to watch her antics were an absolute howl. We fought back the smirks as partway through her trance address she provided us with an advertisement break. One eye opened as the guide said, "This sister is currently unable to get to church because of transport problems. If any drivers are available then please speak to her afterward. You can also speak to her about private sitting and personal auragraphs." She then slipped back into the trance address.

Now don't get me wrong. Although words such as *fruitcake* spring to mind, the medium in question was a lovely, sincere lady but definitely not the Spiritualist medium norm. However, mediums like this do give trance a bad name. Similarly, trance mediumship, sometimes called channeling, also has many surreal practitioners who bring shallow philosophy from grandiose spirits. Some grunt like animals, whistle like dolphins, or give messages from aliens. Perhaps they really are in touch with these beings, for there is no way to prove they are not. But there is no way to prove they are real either.

Trance mediumship, or channeling, can sometimes be a form of self-hypnosis, self-deception, and foolishness. From what I and other sensible witnesses have observed, the real spirit beings that come to speak are humble and disclaim all fame and honor. They have no need for colorful names and lineages. They use their form as a way to identify themselves rather than for glory. They usually speak in the medium's own voice and have no need for mannerisms, gestures, or speaking in an unrecognizable language. The latter exhibitions are almost always the medium's own projections of his or her expectations and desires.

My own trance work developed only after ten years as working as an accurate platform medium, and I insist that the guides who take control give verifiable evidence to prove that the spirit is truly in touch. If this were not the case, there would be no way of knowing that it really is the spirit. It could be my own subconscious speaking or even memories carried forward from past lives. Whether intelligent philosophy or crazy psychobabble is given, it is not proven to be from the spirit unless some form of verification is provided. How else can we test the spirit and know it is true?

So before explaining the function of trance work in a circle I need to prove my point. I have only vague memories about what is said while I am in trance, and for some of my sessions I have no idea who has attended. At an open trance session we had a guest visitor whom none of us knew. "I can remember the evening we had an extraordinary proof from your guide Tara," said Sue from my circle. "The lady you linked to had never been to a trance session before, and the guide told her that she had lost someone very close to her and it was a very sad and painful time for her. This was confirmed. The guide then asked if she minded continuing, as it was obvious that she was still very upset."

I found out later that the woman's name was Vanessa Gates, aged thirty-five, from Fareham, in Hampshire. She was shocked when she spoke to her brother's spirit at the session:

"I heard about Craig and visited his psychic development group in Eastleigh. I was keen to get in touch with my brother, Brian Price, who had died thirteen years ago.

"Sitting in a nearby pitch-dark room waiting to hear the voice of spirit people was a bit like the séances you see in the movies. Soon Craig started speaking to people. His knowledge, he explained, was passed to him by his spirit guide. Eventually I had the courage to ask: 'If someone is murdered, can they tell you who killed them?'

"Craig paused, allowed his guide to overshadow him, then said, 'You are asking because of your brother, Brian, who is with me now. He was murdered in London. They cut his head off.'

"The whole room was stunned. Craig did not know my name and, apart from greeting me when I arrived, had not spoken to me before. What he was saying was shocking—and true. My brother, Brian, had been murdered. Brian, who was thirty-eight, and his girlfriend had been stabbed repeatedly and then had their heads chopped off. He'd been mixing with the wrong types, and the police considered it to be a gangland murder, with drugs involved. The murder has remained unsolved for thirteen years.

"Through the spirit guide, Brian made contact. He told how the murderer had continued to stab his body after he was dead. He mentioned names that I knew had been connected with the inquiry. Brian described how he had died in a dirty flat in a near-derelict block. There was rubbish and broken glass around the room. He said that there was not one murderer but three people present. They came from Bristol, which makes sense, as Brian had lived there. I thought about passing the names he had given to the police, but Brian didn't think his murderers would be punished for what they did to him.

"They will be convicted for other crimes, though, he said. But he made a point of saying he'd died with the first stab to his chest and hadn't suffered. He had watched the events unfold from out of his body. For a long time, I'd been haunted by the thought of him suffering. This put my mind at rest—as did realizing that everyone gets a second chance in the afterlife."

Phill, also from the circle, had a little more to add about the incident: "Tara mentioned that the man who was murdered was dealing drugs out of Bristol and that the people who murdered him were doing business with him when something went wrong. All three of them played a part in his death but the police did not know who had actually killed him. But then Tara gave the three names of the people who were involved in the murder. They were three people who were known to the sitter and also knew her brother. To me this made it an exceptional night and that is why I remember it so long afterward."

If there is a real communication from a spirit guide then they should be able to provide verifiable evidence of the continuation of life. It is my belief that trance mediumship should not be developed until the medium is fully developed as a mental medium. There are a few exceptions in the history of Spiritualism in which evidential trance mediumship has developed in advance of mental mediumship, but I seriously question any form of trance that cannot provide verifiable proof of spirit communication. Students are often eager to try trance work far too soon and before their mental mediumship has flowered. The assumption is that it is easy to channel inspired talk. But the development of trance is dependent on spirit requirements, not personal desires.

Much later in your development the overshadowing by the spirit communicator may increase until it becomes trance. This will happen only if you want it to and if it is the route you choose. Not all mediums are trance mediums. During light trance the medium will be partially conscious and afterward will be able to recall the discourse made by the guide. In deep trance the medium is completely oblivious to what is happening. In most instances the medium's consciousness will shift between light and deep trance, depending upon the need and the available prana energy in the room.

During deep trance, a powerful atmosphere pervades the room as the guide speaks directly through the medium. The guide may tell the sitters things about themselves that can only be know by clairvoyance and may give astonishing spirit proof. When you sit with a true trance medium it is unmistakable that spirit have communicated.

As my circle is primarily a teaching circle, the trance work I do is normally for the purpose of developing the fledgling mediums. The trance teachings are given once the students have advanced enough to understand what is happening and can ask questions of the spirit about their own development and the progress of the group in general. If you are running a circle without a medium then this is something that may not be possible for your group. I must emphasize that trance mediumship should not be developed until the medium has a number of years of provable mental mediumship behind him or her.

As my circle evolves and the sitters develop their mediumistic skills, the spirit guides work through me in trance to prepare the novice mediums to give their first public demonstration. Once the sitters become mediums in their own right then the circle may either disband or continue toward a more advanced stage, perhaps with the development of physical mediumship and accompanying phenomena. I believe that every developed medium should maintain a circle as a permanent part of his spiritual work.

PREPARING FOR THE REAL WORLD

As part of a Spiritualist service the medium is required to give a twenty-minute talk. Sometimes I have a very clear idea of something I would like to talk about but discover that as soon as I open my mouth I deliver a completely different address. I remain in control of myself and would be able to block this if I wanted, but what comes though is far superior to anything I could have planned in advance. Sometimes I am amazed at not only the quality of what is said but also how well planned it is, with a clear beginning, middle, and end.

What I have just described is a very light form of spirit control that we call *inspirational speaking.* My mind is overshadowed and my thoughts are influenced by the spirit guides. In my own case, trance mediumship developed out of inspirational speaking. This next experiment can be introduced when the fledgling mediums are close to being ready to work in the real world. It will prove useful should they need to give an inspired address in a Spiritualist church and it helps them to trust the material being given to them from the spirit.

Step 1: The leader of the group sets a theme for one member of the group to give an inspired address the following week. It is best to have just one speaker at a time to prevent feelings of competitiveness. The theme needs to be fairly open to allow the speaker to improvise and flow with what is given. Some themes may be "hope in adversity," "the brotherhood of man," "the purpose of mediumship," and so on. It is best not to choose as a theme something the speaker is very enthusiastic about, as he or she will enthuse from his or her own mind rather than open to the spirit. For example, if the theme is to talk about angels and the speaker had already read a lot about this and formed preconceptions, then this is likely to get in the way of the flow of ideas given by the spirit.

Step 2: Sometime before the next session, the selected speaker spends time thinking about the theme of the address. He or she can make notes but these should not be read out or used during the address. However, with the theme in mind, I suggest that the speaker have a very simple note prepared that outlines the beginning, middle, and end of the talk. All the speaker needs is a framework. The spirit world will fill in the gaps.

Step 3: At the next meeting the fledgling medium will give his or her address. It is delivered standing and the speaker is encouraged to be as confident as possible. It is better to speak loudly than not loud enough. It is also better to speak slowly rather than quickly.

Step 4: When giving the talk it is good to have a structure, if possible, but it is acceptable to go off subject as long as it is being inspired by spirit. You can talk using your knowledge of the subject, and may include personal anecdotes, but most of all allow the inspiration to shine through. Just as with mediumship, go with the flow. If inspiring words come to you say them. Never apologize if the flow stops or you fumble your words. Just go with it.

Step 5: When the speaker has finished everyone applauds. This not only marks the end of the talk but also instills confidence in the speaker.

I used to be terrified to give an address to an audience but now have no worries about what I say. I know for certain that the spirit world will always be there to help me with the words.

BLINDFOLDED MEDIUMSHIP

Before I send my novice mediums out into the world, I add one more technique to their armory, and that is the ability to make a mediumistic link without knowing who it is for. This is sometimes necessary when working in public as you may not be able to see the person in the audience because of the spotlights or hear them if the microphone is not working. Even in a cozy Spiritualist church people mumble or hide their faces.

This final exercise can be practiced throughout the group's development but is particularly useful in the later stages because reinforces confidence and forces the medium to rely on what he or she intuitively receives from spirit.

Step 1: Two chairs are placed back to back in the center of the circle.

Step 2: Someone is selected to work as the medium. That person sits in one of the chairs and is blindfolded.

Step 3: The circle leader selects someone to be the recipient, who will sit in the other chair with his or her back to the medium. The sitter is chosen in silence and everyone in the room shuffles around making a little noise so that the medium is unable to hear who has sat down.

Step 4: The blindfolded medium is now asked to give a reading for the person sitting behind him or her. It is particularly good if the medium can make a link with the spirit but he or she may start on a psychic level if necessary.

Step 5: The recipient of the messages remains silent throughout and indicates to the group leader what is correct by using head nods, hand gestures, and facial expressions. The group leader must give nothing away when transmitting the recipient's answers aloud, including the gender of the recipient. For example, the medium may say, "This person has a grandmother in the spirit with the name of Mary." Then, depending on the answer, the circle leader may say something like, "The person in the chair is indicating that this is correct." By working in this way the medium has to rely entirely on their impressions. There are no voice tones or other clues to make the link work.

Step 6: When finished, the recipient of the messages explains what facts were right and which were wrong. There are likely to be a few things that were hard to give a definitive yes or no answer to, so these may need explaining. For example, the Mary link given as an example in step 5 may have been correct, but the spirit was the aunt not the grandmother.

9 PRESENTATION: WORKING WITH AN AUDIENCE

"When an audience do not complain, it is a compliment, and when they do it is a compliment, too, if unaccompanied by violence."
—Mark Twain

Whether a medium is demonstrating in front of a dozen people or performing at a packed theater, it is important that the mediumship is presented in a clear and interesting way. The medium must give the audience an understanding of who the spirit communicator is, what kind of information verifies that it is the purported spirit, and what the spirit has to say to the recipient. The medium also needs to speak clearly and with confidence and to know certain spiritual skills, such as moving with the energy of the audience.

Many new mediums shudder at the prospect of standing in front of an audience. They fear the spirit will not come though. They fear they will freeze and humiliate themselves. They fear their gift will not work outside of the circle. They are wrong. The quality of clairvoyance may sometimes vary, but experienced mediums know that spirit will never let them down. If spirit communicators can come through in a circle for one person, they also can come through when you demonstrate in front of millions.

If and when your time comes to step in front of an audience, have no fear and do not be unduly concerned if you are trembling like a leaf. All this adrenalin actually helps focus the mind and spirit. The psychic power of the audience will lift your mediumship to new heights. It is easier than working in circle. And the bigger the crowd, the easier it gets.

HOW TO DRESS

It was once the case that there was nothing more frightening to the Establishment than a hippie in a suit. It was unnerving because the danger was that people might take them seriously. Similarly, many consider people psychics and mediums to be on the fringe of society. The skeptics feel more comfortable if mediums wear big earrings, brightly colored vests, sequined jackets, or ostentatious dresses. These are the Madam Zazas or the Gypsy Acorahs from the fairgrounds, and nobody is going to take them seriously. Skeptics sneer at them and can easily dismiss them as entertainers or cranks. But a medium who dresses with polish rings the alarm bells: "Be careful of this one!"

I like to dress like the Establishment. Most other mediums working in television today also dress smartly and project a fashionable, modern air. This is the way it should be. No smoking dry ice. No ghost-buster music. We don't want to look like characters from fairy stories nor do we want to look like a 1950s Spiritualist. We do want to look professional and confident. We have something of value to offer the world. Mediumship is not entertainment. Mediumship challenges science. Mediumship challenges religion. Mediumship is a very serious business that we present in a spirit of cheerfulness and compassion. People are beginning to take it seriously. Dress well and people's attitudes toward you change.

HOW TO PRESENT YOURSELF

It is likely that you will feel nervous when you first stand in front of even a small group to give your demonstration of mediumship. This is quite natural and shows that you care about doing well. Prior to you demonstration of mediumship you would have meditated, and the underlying peacefulness imparted by this state will continue working in the background of your awareness. When you stand up to speak allow this relaxed state to stay with you and transform your nervousness into vitality and enthusiasm.

During the meditation before the demonstration you may want to include a visualization of yourself giving a first-class demonstration of mediumship. See yourself speaking in a loud, understandable, assured voice with clear information coming through from the spirit. Know also that the audience wants you to do well. As a medium you will sense their energy and support and this will bolster your self-confidence.

The rest is up to the spirit people. You may have a loose idea of the things you want to say but in my opinion it is best to just go with the flow and let spirit do the work. There is no need to plan in detail what you are going to say or have any prepared messages to give. The right words will come if you open yourself to the guidance of the spirit. Allow the spirit helpers to inspire you and speak from the heart. Interact with your audience, and particularly with the person receiving the message. Occasionally you may joke with the audience and talk with them as if they are your personal friends. Encourage them speak back to you and ask them to explain why they are accepting some of the strange information you give them. This will make the demonstration more interactive and, therefore, more interesting.

Most important is that the you and audience hear the voice of the person receiving the message. It is an essential part of the demonstration and it helps the mediumship to work. Tell the recipient at the start that you need to hear his or her voice and, if necessary, badger that person to speak up while you are doing the reading. Someone nodding at you is not much help. Like you, the audience wants to know if what you are saying is being accepted—and they want to hear it being confirmed. If necessary, repeat back the person's mumbled answer so that the audience is aware that the message is being accepted.

Some mediums believe that the voice is a "fluence"—a vibration link that helps the energy to flow between the medium and the sitter. Nonetheless, when we demonstrate mediumship in my Internet chat room we get good results even though there is no voice to work with. Also, I have given evidential demonstrations to academics and skeptics during which it was agreed nobody except me would speak to prove that I was being guided by voice tone. The bottom line is that the voice is not essential during a demonstration but it helps. I certainly feel that sometimes the voice helps me to connect to the recipient and, consequently, that our auras become connected. Verbal responses are a sure way to know that your messages are being accepted, and it is far more satisfying and friendly to have this interaction with the audience.

Deliver your mediumship with cheerfulness, compassion, and enthusiasm. If something does go wrong, don't worry and don't make apologies; this will only draw attention to something the members of the audience may not have noticed. Instead concentrate on the mediumship. Listen to the inner voice and relay your messages. In this way the focus of your attention will shift away from your anxieties and toward your mediumship, making it easy for you to project with confidence to your audience.

THE CERT RULE

CERT is a teaching method used by many mediums and one we apply at my online psychic school. The term was coined by my good friend and superb medium Stephen O'Brien, who speaks about it in his book *The Power of Your Spirit*. CERT is an acronym that stands for the four elements that make up a good reading, and when used as a tool for demonstration, it determines a sensible order in which these elements can be presented.

The CERT rule can be applied during one-on-one consultations but becomes particularly important when demonstrating to an audience. CERT is a simple way to package your mediumship so that the message is clear and has structure. It will make it much easier for the recipient to identify the spirit communicator and it gives you a framework to guide your mediumship. Not all mediums use this method and I, too, will often work in completely different ways to this, but it is certainly a good way to get started and is a reliable method that is often in the back of my mind when demonstrating.

CERT stands for these components:
C = Communicator
E = Evidence
R = Reason
T = Tie it up

C = Communicator
As I have said often in these pages, the objective of mediumship is to prove the survival of the human personality after death. Therefore, it is important that the recipient knows which spirit is communicating with him or her. Normally this is a relative, a loved one, or friend who is well-know to the sitter and easily identified. However, sometimes unexpected people come through, such as old school friends, acquaintances, or relatives with messages for people you know. Sometimes two spirit people, such as a married couple, will try to communicate with the medium at the same time, causing a crossed line that can be confusing to sort out. If we can establish exactly who is giving the message, then there is much less room for confusion.

My mediumship has developed to the point where I can usually give the Christian name and surname of the spirit communicator, but this is not always the case—and certainly was not the case when I started out. If we do not know the communicator's name then we need to build the identity of the spirit using other pieces of information. I have covered some of these points already, but it does no harm to summarize the essentials.

You will probably be aware from the onset if the communicator is a man, woman, or child. This may be the first information you give. You may also add details about the spirit's appearance: height, weight, and build; color of hair, skin and eyes; age; and any other details that come to you. Most significant is that you may sense how the spirit died and what illnesses were dominant at the end. This is important because the illnesses at the end are among the most enduring and upsetting memories the recipient has of the person who died. From this information you will know if the spirit communicator is a friend or a family member. Using clairaudience you may also intuit their name, but do not worry unduly if this does not come. This is the icing on the cake, the important thing is that you have established who is communicating and everyone now knows from whom the message is coming.

E = Evidence

You have established the communicator, now you can punch the message home. This is the point where you can ask the spirit to give you further evidence that he or she is really the person he or she claims to be. All sorts of information will be given to you by the spirit communicator to help qualify who they are. You may include information about their mannerisms, idiosyncrasies, and events happening in the family or in the recipient's life. You will talk about shared memories and perhaps recount memorable events from the past, some of which may be very personal and known only to the recipient. There will also be things you will say that make no sense to anyone listening but are very important to the person receiving the message.

If you give exactly what you are given by the spirit communicator, your messages will be filled with tremendous detail and accuracy.

R = Reason

Now that the proof has been given and we know that it really is the spirit of the loved one giving the message, we now ask the spirit to tell us the reason they have made the link today. The reason may be quite simple, such as to give emotional support, to give hope and comfort, or to let the recipient know that they are not alone and that their loved ones in spirit are aware of what is happening to them.

While the primary focus of all mediumship is to provide evidence that the human personality continues after death, sometimes the spirit communicator will also give a bonus and advise the sitter about issues and situations surrounding them. In a private consultation this may be detailed but in a public demonstration this may be abridged to a few simple messages of hope and reassurance and simple advice about what is best to do. This information will not include predictions about the future.

T = Tie It Up

Now you need to conclude your reading so that you can move on to the next person. Every reading is like a short story with a beginning, middle, and an end. By tying up the reading with a simple conclusion it gives everyone watching a feeling of satisfaction that there has been resolution. If there are any loose ends, such as parts of a message that were not initially understood, then now is a good time to sort these out.

The conclusion of the reading needs to be concise: It may be simply a message from the spirit communicator to say "I love you." However, since people tend to remember the first thing you say and the last thing you say, I try to make the conclusion strong. I usually include a précis of some of the most evidential facts that have already been accepted, such as the name of the communicator and the salient facts I have discovered about him or her. For example, "You father, Charles Kinsley, sends his love to you and wants you to remember some of the things he said today by way of proof, such as . . . He also brings forward the love of the others who have linked today, including Betty Williams from the dairy, Fred Chapman, who had the bad legs, . . . " and so on.

This hammers home the evidence and gives a summary that will be remembered. Then end by asking the spirit for an uplifting message of hope and relay this to the recipient. In this way you leave the link on a positive note, you hold the audience's attention, and the energy remains high as you move on to the next person.

WORKING WITH AN AUDIENCE

When the members of a circle are ready to begin demonstrating, the medium leading the circle will usually plan a "fledgling demonstration." If the medium comes from a Spiritualist background then this is normally arranged at a Spiritualist center, and the audience already will know how mediumship works and be sympathetic and less critical than a paying general audience.

The first time I set foot in a Spiritualist church was as a fledgling medium.

Peter Close, our circle leader, prepared us in the weeks leading up to the event and worked with us to refine our gifts in readiness for the specific tasks each of us was to perform. One of us would do the opening prayer, another would give a short inspired address, some would demonstrate psychometry, and a few would demonstrate mediumship. Shaking like leaves, we stood in front of the sea of eyes and took turns demonstrating our gifts. To our astonishment it worked. We could do it! In fact, afterward members of the audience approached us to say that our mediumship was better than they had seen from mediums who had been working most of their lives—and they were not just being nice, then meant it.

Working in Spiritualist churches is easy for both fledgling and more advanced mediums because the energy is usually high and the congregation is normally open-minded and used to watching mediums work. Spiritualists will still demand evidence but will be more tolerant than the general public and understanding when things go awry. When working with large public audiences the medium usually needs to be more dynamic and a bit of a showman.

The methods I am about to discuss will help you to deliver your messages with energy and make your work interesting to watch should you eventually demonstrate at larger venues. Much of what follows also will apply when working one-on-one, and I advise trainees about these same criteria when they demonstrate their skills in my online psychic chat rooms.

Establishing an Empathy with the Audience
People who have paid to watch you in a theater are expecting to be entertained. Of course mediums are not entertainers, we are doing an important spiritual task, but if we are to reach the general public we need to go out into the world and present ourselves to them. A television producer once advised me to be myself when I go on air but be a slightly magnified version of myself. In other words, you have to consciously project your personality but at the same time do not ham it up or make yourself look false or silly.

In the case of a live audience, you have to get them on your side. This can be done by talking with sincerity and compassion and also instilling a little humor. This can happen right from the start, but it works best when injected into the mediumship part of the demonstration. I may say things such as "I want to come to the man with the blue aura with yellow spots," or "I want to come to the lady with the ghastly pink cardigan," or I may point in some vague direction and say, "I want to come to the lady on this side, the lady with the strong features." I will not actually identify whom I am talking about, but playing with the audience like this can sometimes lift the energy. You have to be careful, of course not to overstep the mark, as some people may not see the joke or take you literally and your tongue in cheek remarks may be taken as insults!

Most mediums have a few silly comments up their sleeve that they throw in when the energy needs a lift. It's one of the things that makes mediumship fun to do and fun to watch. Although we are dealing with some very sensitive issues and tragedies, a little humor will help to lift the grief and allow the energy to flow. Laughter can sometimes be an expression of love.

The first links that you make are also very important because from these you establish your ability and get the audience's trust and, with it, their support and energy. If the first link goes wrong it may take some time to get the energy flowing again. You need to have the audience's belief and confidence, which creates a sort of energy that will work in your favor. Actors and actresses know that an audience has its own energy, which can lift or floor the performer.

The First Link

Mediums are often asked, "How do you know who to go to when giving a link to an audience?" The truth is that most of the time we have absolutely no idea until we start speaking. In my own case, I find the first link of the evening is given to me as I stand up from my chair or step onto the stage. Spirit usually gives me a name, but only at the last minute and just before I am to speak. It can be nerve-wracking, as I do not know if I am tuned in or linked to spirit at all until I actually start working.

This is where advance clairvoyance comes in handy. Sometimes a communicator may link to the medium the day before the show, and this information can be explained to the audience just before you work. I remember watching the great medium Doris Stokes work, and she started her session by saying that a name had come to her while being driven to the show. It was impressive when she added a long list of details and someone in the audience affirmed all of it. Advance clairvoyance can be arresting to people who have never witnessed it, for it cannot be explained away by cold reading, fishing for information, watching facial expressions, telepathy, or listening to voice tones.

Sometimes a name and other details will come to me prior to giving a demonstration, but normally I do not get the link until the moment I am about to speak. Other times there is a name on my mind but it is completely overwritten when it comes to the actual demonstration. The truth is that every medium works in a different way, and no one way is better than another. Some may give wonderful factual evidence, such as names and dates, but may miss some of the intimate and heartfelt information. For others the reverse may apply. What matters is that the recipient and the audience understand that a spirit person has made a connection and added a little more to the evidence suggesting life after death.

Moving with the Flow

When you stand in front of an audience you will be aware of their energy and will be drawn to certain areas of the auditorium or to individual people. Most of the time you will not be able to resist the pull of this energy and may find yourself giving messages to people all over the place—sometimes including people waiting in the wings, in the bar, or in the entrance area. In these instances you'll have to send someone out to get them!

This is a sign of the spirit's determination to get a message through to specific people, but as a medium you have a lot more control than you may at first think. While doing a demonstration you can simultaneously have an inward conversation with your spirit helpers and ask for their help. If, for example, you notice the energy in the room is dropping you can suggest that they bring a cheerful link through—a communicator who will lift the energy by making people laugh. Who comes though is usually outside of your control, but the guides will pay attention and help you with links that will enable things to move smoothly. While the guides are lining up the communicators, it is you who are standing in front of an audience and it is your judgment that counts. So if you feel you need help, ask the spirit guides—they will help only if you ask them.

If audience is vibrant and receptive, the energy will be like a liquid light flowing from place to place. When the energy is really high you may see it like a lake of light that moves around the auditorium. If you cannot place a link you are describing, submit to the energy and let it guide you. You may be drawn to a specific area or to a particular seat and, in some instances, you may see a bright light around the person who is to have the message. Invariably when cross-examined he or she will turn out to be the recipient, or, if it is not that person, then it is someone sitting very near. It may be that the potential receiver is shy or hesitates to come forward. Perhaps the receiver could place some of the information, but needs additional details before acknowledging it all.

As the one in control of the demonstration, it is possible for you to work with the spirit communicators to line up the next link while you are finishing the first one. When doing this, make sure you move around the audience. If you give messages only to one section of the audience you will lose the attention of the rest—and with it goes their energy and the power that drives you. So if you have a link at the front of the hall, make the next link at the back or up in the balcony. In this way the audience will need to turn around to see to whom you are speaking, which makes the experience more active and interesting. It also keeps everyone alert, as no one knows to whom you are going to go next. It could be anyone, and so they remain expectant and excited if they do eventually get connected.

Getting Unstuck

There will inevitably be times when you are stuck, a link is not spoken for. This can be very disconcerting, but do not let it unnerve you. Whatever happens, do not apologize, for this will only undermine the good work you are doing. The reason a link has not been made is usually because the person in the audience has heard everything but has not yet made the connection to him- or herself. A name you said may have thrown the receiver off the link, or he or she may not want to accept the message in such a public place.

Don't abandon the link unless you are absolutely forced to do so. With a little perseverance you can usually find the person the message is for. You may be drawn to that person by the energy in the room, but in some cases it may require you to clarify your information. Don't panic. Summarize what you have so far and remind the audience that you may have a name wrong or the actual name may sound similar to the one you have. Often the audience does not realize the subtle nature of mediumship—they assume you are like a crystal-clear telephone line to the other side. Any genuine medium will know that this is simply not the case. Wires get crossed and the signal is sometimes muffled, so do not be too proud to admit the link may be fuzzy. Nonetheless, the odds are that you are probably one hundred percent right but that the recipient for the message has not been found yet.

Persevere but do not force the message on someone. I would rather accept I have not placed a link than give the message to someone who is trying to be helpful or making the link fit. Until you are completely sure the link is right, keep the options for whom it is with open. When the link is truly found you will know it for certain. You will have an unmistakable gut feeling that it is right. Then when the connection is made you will not only be able to place the information correctly but will also find that even more details will flow.

Of course, there always will be the difficult audience members. You may get what we mediums call a "message grabber"—someone who will try to grab every message you give as their own in the hope that a real message will eventually come through for them. These people are a hazard because they will accept the initial message and then retract partway through in order to move you to a real link for themselves. The spirit communicators will have no choice but to go quiet on you. Be aware that this can sometimes happen and try to identify this sort of person at the onset. Politely say that you feel you are not with him or her and move on to find the real recipient of the message.

You may also get what we call a "blocker." Every audience has at least one of these prove-it-to-me receivers, people who want to make the medium work as hard as possible in the hope that the message they get will be more detailed. They may also try to hold the medium by being awkward, such as initially accepting everything and then refuting some information that has already been accepted as correct. In this way they hold the medium's attention and wrongly assume that by not letting you leave them they will get a more detailed message. You will also find blockers very tiring to work with and their selfishness may drain your energy. I drop them as quickly as I can, but I make sure that I leave them on a high note. Once they have accepted a good piece of evidence, I conclude quickly and say I have a link for someone else. Some people have their own petty agenda and it is not worth wasting your precious energy with them. There are likely to be far more deserving people in the audience who will benefit from your expertise. Move on and don't feel guilty about being forced to break a link. Public work is there for everyone to enjoy.

Trusting the Spirit

There may be occasions when the message is correct but you are trying to give it to the wrong person. When this happens ask the audience if anyone there can understand most of the link. Again, one small detail may be throwing things out of whack, so you may need to put that aside and sort the rest out toward the end of the message, once the flow is going well. By that time the true receiver may have remembered the detail they initially could not accept. You may be mistaken, of course, but in the majority of instances everything you have been given is right but you have gotten into a tangle with the context.

You have to believe in yourself and trust the information you are being given when you work in public. In the early days of your mediumship it is particularly difficult to give information that appears to be ridiculous, but you will be surprised when it is accepted. One of the first demonstrations I did alone, without the support of the circle or my medium mentor, required me to give what appeared to be a nonsensical message. The spirit showed me an image of Long John Silver with a wooden leg, hook, and a parrot on his shoulder and impressed me to tell a rather grumpy-looking man at the back of the audience what I was seeing. This was my first time at the venue and I wanted to be accurate, but was very concerned that I may make myself look like a complete fool. Nonetheless I gave the message.

"I have someone here who wants to link to you. He is dressed like Long John Silver from *Treasure Island*." Then some more information came to me once I had the courage to give what I got. "And he says his name is Peter. I believe he is your uncle."

"Oh yes, that's my uncle Peter," replied the man, his face now breaking into a smile. "It's not Long John Silver, it's Captain Hook you are seeing. Uncle Peter used to work in pantomime and would play the character regularly at the Christmas show!"

Can you imagine the relief that came when I got that right? Remember, this was one of my first demonstrations out on my own, and the spirit helpers really threw me in at the deep end with that message. It was sink or swim. And I swam.

The more you trust the spirit communicators the more accurate your mediumship will become. Nowadays I have all sorts of strange messages come through, and some can be very odd indeed. For example, I once gave a message from a spirit who's head had been cryogenically frozen. "A complete waste of money!" was the spirit's comment. I have relayed secret symbolism from the Grand Lodge by a "dead" Freemason—though I wonder how it is possible to keep any form of secret in the spirit world. I have had spirits show themselves dressed in the uniform of the Queen of England's Coldstream guards, with flamboyant red tunic and bearskin busby. And I have had spirit communicators who have shown me everything from bagpipes to Kango hammers to identify who they are.

If we can give unusual facts that can be verified only by the recipient and no one else in the theater, it helps to negate the skeptics' accusation that all mediums give cold readings: that we give information that could apply to anyone or that can easily be made to fit with what the recipient wants to hear. We mediums need to give this level of irrefutable proof, which comes by trusting the spirit. If you have the courage to say what the spirit impresses on your mind, your mediumship will become more accurate. Sometimes we will make mistakes and our own unconscious thoughts will get muddled with what the spirits are trying to tell us. We may look foolish, but does that really matter? The fact that we may get some things wrong reveals our honesty. In time you will find that your accuracy will come close to one hundred percent right, but this will happen only if you trust what you are being given by the spirit.

Dead Ends

If you do come up against a brick wall of one sort or another when demonstrating, there are a few things you can do to help yourself:

Perhaps the recipient does not understand mediumship.
Just because the person receiving the message has come to see a medium, it doesn't necessarily follow that he or she is open to receiving a message. It may be the receiver's first time to a demonstration or perhaps he or she gave someone a lift, are theater staff, or has been reluctantly dragged along by a partner. If there is neither the desire nor the need to know, then you will probably only be able to work on a psychic level for these people.

Others may be shy, very upset, or be concerned that you will reveal all of their secrets to the world. You may need to give reassurance or simplify what you are doing. For example, I described someone in great detail to a sitter who, to my dismay, rejected all of it, saying, "It's all nonsense, what you say. The person you are describing is dead!" Clearly she had no idea what a medium does.

Perhaps a detail has thrown the receiver off.
People think that a medium is like a telephone line to the next world and will assume that everything you say is true and that you make no mistakes. They may be able to accept most of what you have given but then a detail, such as the name, is not understood and they then assume the whole link is wrong.

If this happens, ask them to put the name aside for a while and continue with the evidence. If the link is still proving to be correct, you can tie up the loose ends at the end or at some point during the communication. Postponing takes off the pressure and, so long as it is the correct link, allows your flow to continue. People have bad memories and sometimes it takes a little while for the penny to drop. Usually this happens during the demonstration, and the information is finally accepted, but do not blame yourself if after trying to tie up the loose ends it isn't accepted. Invariably the person will approach you afterward to say he or she has remembered or made a cell-phone call to someone who confirmed it.

Perhaps your energy is low.
When you are working you will sometimes become so enthusiastic that you do not realize how spiritually tired you are becoming. After a number of good links you may suddenly hit a brick wall. This may occur if your energy has dropped or the energy of the audience has dropped.

If this happens, pace yourself. Drink some water and say something to the audience—a few sentences about what you are doing or something to make them laugh. Getting the audience's interest will lift the energy. After this very short pause you can return to the sitter and work psychically for a while. For example, you may tell the sitter something about his or her aura colors or about any current issues surrounding him or her. Mention that you are working on a psychic level while your energy is replenishing. Once the flow is back you can return to mediumship and give the same recipient information about their spirit loved ones.

Perhaps you have more than one spirit communicator.
If the spirit people are keen to communicate, they can sometimes clamber over one another to get through. As the medium, you are stuck in the middle with more than one communicator giving you information. If you sense this, point out that there may be more than one communicator and sort out the information. For example, the person may know two people named Frank and both come through together. Explain the differences between them so that the recipient understands who you are describing.

Occasionally you may find yourself with two similar links for two different people. Again distinguish who's who and then settle on a reading for just one of the recipients. When you have finished, you may decide to return to the link that was uncertain and give another message. Doing this satisfies both recipients and clearly shows that you leave no loose ends.

Perhaps you are on a dead link.
If the information is definitely not being taken from the person you originally connected to, you may need to look elsewhere for the link. The recipient is most likely to be sitting somewhere near the original link. You will probably feel drawn to the right person, but if not ask if anyone else in that vicinity can take what you have given. It is likely that with perseverance you will find the right person and everything will be taken.

If the link is not taken by anyone and you just cannot place it, then thank the spirit for trying and move on. It may take a while to get back into your stride but you'll have no choice but to continue. Try not to let the lost link upset you. On the occasions it has happened to me, the link was invariably placed afterward by someone who was either too embarrassed or too mean-spirited to put up his or her hand.

If you stumble while working, do not blame yourself or apologize; instead move on. It is a waste of time to embroil yourself on the one wrong link. If you follow the advice given above, you will rarely get into this situation, but if you do, do not punish yourself. Every honest medium has had difficult demonstrations some time in their work. It is the fake "mediums" who get it right all of the time. Remember, it is not your fault, nor the fault of the spirit, if something is not taken. Real mediums make a few mistakes—it shows that you are true.

Go Forward

Becoming a medium usually requires a certain amount of sacrifice. Certainly we have to sacrifice our preconceptions, but many of us have to make radical and often difficult adjustments to our lives as mediums. I sometimes wonder whether mediums have to experience the full blow of adversity so they learn to sympathize with loss and grief. A hard experience will often inspire a sensitive person to help others in need.

Despite the sincerity and dedication of so many mediums, a large number of "sensible people" still sneer at us, and mainstream society and the media still consider Spiritualism and the like to be a dubious fringe belief system. There remains a great deal of prejudice toward our kind and I am sure that for a long time to come skeptics will continue to scoff and religious individuals will continue to condemn us. Know that being a medium is not an easy path and inevitably there will be times when you will be standing alone against the forces of ignorance. Be prepared to stick by your beliefs, and no matter how hard it gets never give up.

There will be many times when you do not see the good you have accomplished through your work, but eventually you will receive testimonials from people whom you have helped. It is likely that the most important facts you give are those you do not think are startling evidence. It is the small details that clinch it and turn the course for the sitter. An example happened just recently during one of Jane's consultations. Jane couldn't understand why the sitter sobbed for so long when she said that she saw the woman's "dead" mother holding a tin of a polish called Brasso. It transpired that the word *Brasso* was the deathbed code the sitter and her mother had agreed would be the proof that the spirit was she. So you see, a medium never knows just how much is contained in just a single word.

What a joy it is to be able to prove for certain that life is eternal. What courage and hope it brings to the desperate to know that we need have no fear of death. What an inspiration it is to know for certain that one day we will once again meet those we loved and who we thought that death had taken from us. The philosophy we learn from this is that we are immortal beings on a pilgrimage through eternity. We are part of a cosmic process of becoming that may extend over many lifetimes. This knowledge changes everything, for not only do we see death differently but life also takes on new meaning.

ABOUT THE AUTHOR

Craig Hamilton-Parker is a British author, television personality and professional psychic medium. He is best known for his TV shows *Our Psychic Family*, *The Spirit of Diana* and *Nightmares Decoded*. On television he usually works with his wife Jane Hamilton-Parker who is also a psychic medium. Their work was showcased in a three part documentary on the BBC called *Mediums Talking to the Dead*.

They now have TV shows in the USA and spend a lot of time demonstrating mediumship around the world.

Born in Southampton UK, Craig was convinced at an early age that he was mediumistic. He became a well known as a platform medium within Spiritualism and in 1994 left his job as advertising executive to become the resident psychic on Channel 4 television's *The Big Breakfast* making predictions for upcoming news stories. He wrote a regular psychic advice column for *The Scottish Daily Record* and regular features for *The Daily Mail*, *Sunday Mirror* and *The People*.

His first book about the psychic genre was published in 1995 and are now published in many languages.

You can find out more and join Craig & Jane's work and Spiritual Foundation at their website: **psychics.co.uk**

PUBLISHED BOOKS

Hamilton-Parker, Craig & Jane (1995) *The Psychic Workbook* Random House ISBN 0-09-179086-7 (Languages: English, Chinese)

Hamilton-Parker, Craig (1996) *Your Psychic Powers* Hodder & Stoughton ISBN 0-340-67417-2 (Languages: English)

Hamilton-Parker, Craig (1999) *Timeless Wisdom of the Tibetans* Hodder & Stoughton ISBN 0-340-70483-7 (Languages: English)

Hamilton-Parker, Craig (1999) *The Psychic Casebook* Blandford/Sterling ISBN 0-7137-2755-1 (Languages: English, Turkish)

Hamilton-Parker, Craig (1999) *The Hidden Meaning of Dreams* Sterling imprint Barnes & Noble ISBN 0-8069-7773-6 (Languages: English, Spanish, Portuguese, Russian, Israeli, Greek Icelandic.)

Hamilton-Parker, Craig (2000) *The Intuition Pack* Godfield Books ISBN 1-84181-007-X

Hamilton-Parker, Craig (2000) *Remembering Your Dreams* Sterling imprint Barnes & Noble ISBN 0-8069-4343-2

Hamilton-Parker, Craig (2000) *Unlock Your Secret Dreams* Sterling imprint Barnes & Noble ISBN 1-4027-0316-3

Hamilton-Parker, Craig (2002) *Fantasy Dreaming* Sterling imprint Barnes & Noble ISBN 0-8069-5478-7

Hamilton-Parker, Craig (2003) *Protecting the Soul* Sterling imprint Barnes & Noble ISBN 0-8069-8719-7

Hamilton-Parker, Craig (2004) *Psychic Dreaming* Sterling imprint Barnes & Noble ISBN 1-4027-0474-7

Hamilton-Parker, Craig (2005) *Opening to the Other Side* Sterling imprint Barnes & Noble ISBN 1-4027-1346-0

Hamilton-Parker, Craig (2010) *What To Do When You Are Dead* Sterling imprint Barnes & Noble ISBN 978-1-4027-7660-1 (Languages: English, Dutch, Portuguese)

NEW: WHAT IF THE FUTURE COULD BE PREDICTED WITH 100% ACCURACY?

Messages from the Universe reveals the secrets of the lost Indian oracle that can predict the future with 100% accuracy - including the exact time of your death. Its 5,000 year old pages had Craig's name written on it together with a message that its secrets can now be revealed to the world. Read this incredible account of how the oracle revealed mind-boggling information about Craig's past lives, present life and his future incarnations and how the oracle also contains information about the future of the world.

Available from: psychics.co.uk

ONLINE PSYCHIC SCHOOL

At our Online Psychic School we have classes, courses and circles happening most week days as well as a thriving community of spiritually minded people.

Join our Online Psychic School: psychics.co.uk

CLAIRVOYANCE SERVICES

Craig & Jane Hamilton-Parker offer psychic and mediumistic readings from their website. They also have an online community where you can ask questions and share your paranormal dreams and psychic insights with like minded people.

Visit: psychics.co.uk

If you would like a reading today you can call their telephone psychics and book a reading on the numbers below:

UK: 0800 067 8600
USA: 1855 444 6887
EIRE: 1800 719 656
AUSTRALIA: 1800 825 305

Callers must be 18 or over to use this service and have the bill payers permission. For entertainment purposes only. All calls are recorded. PhonePayPlus regulated SP: StreamLive Ltd, EC4R 1BB, 0800 0673 330.

Printed in the USA
CPSIA information can be obtained
at www.ICGtesting.com
LVHW010036280124
770146LV00011B/1060

9 781502 477989